A HISTORY OF BRIXTON

by Alan Piper

KU-289-765

Published by the Brixton Society

BRIXTON CHALLENGE

ABOUT THE AUTHOR

Alan Piper was born in Brixton in 1947. He qualified as a member of the RIBA in 1978 and worked as principal architect for Lewisham Borough Council. In 1993 he joined the Board of Brixton Challenge as the representative of local community groups.

He is very active in local affairs including being Secretary of the Brixton Sheltered Street Scheme, Chairman of the Lambethans and Secretary of the Brixton Society; and is well known as a lecturer to local schools and at the Lambeth Archives Open Days.

Published by the Brixton Society, 82 Mayall Road, London SE24 0PJ. General enquiries to Alan Piper (Secretary) on (0171) 207 0347. Designed and produced by Barnes Vereker.

© The Brixton Society 1996, all rights reserved.
A catalogue record for this book is available from the British Library.
ISBN 1 873052 07 3

Front cover picture: Lambeth Town Hall, opened in 1908, and the Budd Memorial of 1824. (Richard Barnatt/Brixton Challenge).

Printed in Great Britain.

CONTENTS

BRIXTON SOCIETY PUBLICATIONS

Any of the following publications by the Brixton Society mentioned in this book may be obtained from:

The Brixton Society Archivist
32 Stockwell Green
London SW9 9HZ

Prices are:

ISBN	TITLE	PRICE	P&P*
1 873052 00 6	Brixton Town Trails	£3.99	25p
1 873052 01 4	Brixton the Story of a Name	£1.00	25p
1 873052 02 2	Effra: Lambeth's Underground River	£1.50	25p
1 873052 03 0	Trams in Brixton 1870-1951	50p	25p
1 873052 04 9	Stockwell Congregational School	30p	25p
1 873052 05 7	Most Agreeable Suburb	15p	25p
1 873052 06 5	Brixton Memories	£4.99	50p
1 873052 07 3	A History of Brixton	£9.99	50p

Where more than one item is ordered, the maximum post and packaging for an order is £1.

Please make cheques payable to "The Brixton Society".

Lambeth Town Hall (Richard Barnatt, Brixton Challenge)

INTRODUCTION

Like any other local amenity society, the Brixton Society takes a keen interest in local history, but our active involvement in planning, conservation and community issues during the past 20 years has overshadowed this aspect of our work. Fortunately, in recent years there has been more agreement among local interests about the future of Brixton, so we have gradually been able to devote more time to researching and publishing information about its past.

Until now, no general history of the Brixton area has been available to the public, and anyone wishing to research a particular aspect of Brixton has had no historical framework to start from. This has been frustrating both to schoolteachers trying to help their pupils to understand their surroundings, and to specialists who have found it easier to apply their expertise elsewhere.

Lambeth's early historians focussed on the Thames riverside, and with no great battles or ancient monuments to discuss, paid little attention to the hinterland. Unlike Streatham or Clapham, Brixton did not grow from an old village with continuity of parish or manor records. Instead it developed very rapidly during the 19th century from a few quiet hamlets into a busy commercial centre surrounded by populous new suburbs. Our street plan as we know it today was largely completed by the outbreak of the First World War, although since then the district has seen many other changes.

All this means that we have had to build up the story from all manner of original material, archives, maps and reminiscences. Different sources don't always agree and some parts of the story have been difficult to trace at all. On the other hand, we have had to radically simplify a surfeit of material on some issues, in order to keep the book to a manageable size. It was always our intention to provide an introductory history which would stimulate interest and encourage others to find out more, so we have included details of further reading as an appendix, together with a basic index. As for pictures, we have tried to cover a broader timespan than the familiar Edwardian postcard views, and managed to reach back another century earlier.

Although it has been left to me to weave all the material into a coherent narrative, many others have contributed to the research and production of this book. Far and away the greatest share of the research was provided by the late Ken Dixon, who obtained old maps, investigated individual buildings, and located key documents from the Society's own accumulation of papers. Since his death in January 1995, the support and co-operation of the staff at Lambeth Archives has been crucial in filling gaps and providing most of the illustrations. Finally, we are immensely grateful to Brixton Challenge Co.Ltd., both for their financial support in realising this long-standing project, and for their patience during frequent redrafting as new facts were unearthed.

Alan Piper

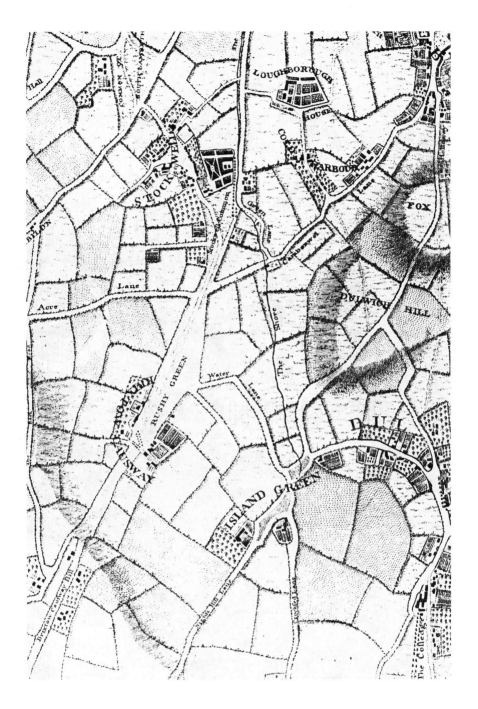

Rural Brixton: part of Rocque's map of 1745 – not wholly accurate, but the present centre is clearly shown as common land. (Lambeth Archives)

8

CHAPTER 1 - RURAL BRIXTON

1.1 Origins

The earliest surviving buildings in our part of Lambeth date from the late 18th century, when what is now Brixton was still largely farmland, with isolated buildings along the few roads. Fortunately, enough buildings have survived to illustrate all stages of its development since then. From earlier times, though, the only traces are to be found in certain road lines, plot boundaries, and in the main, old documents.

The earliest surviving traces of human activity are the lines of two Roman Roads, now Clapham Road (the A3) and Brixton Road (the A23).

Of the two, Clapham Road was probably the more important Roman highway, linking the City of London with the port of Chichester and a fort near Portsmouth. The other road took a more southerly route, leading to a network of small-scale iron workings in Sussex, but no evidence has yet come to light of any Roman settlements along Brixton Road or Brixton Hill.

During Roman times, these roads doubtless brought trade, but after the collapse of the Roman Empire, they were more likely to bring trouble from marauding war bands looking for loot. The pattern that then emerged consisted of small farming communities, sited away from these main roads. Thus a small hamlet developed around what became Stockwell Green, midway between the two roads.

In the later years of the Roman Empire, the Imperial Army was increasingly supplemented by Germanic mercenaries, paid by allotting them land which they could farm to support themselves. After the last Roman troops left in 407 AD, the British authorities relied on the same policy to resist Irish raids from the West. Bands of warriors were recruited from Germany and initially given lands in East Kent.

Once these mercenaries decided to fight on their own behalf, the Roman Province of Britain rapidly fragmented into many small territories, each controlled by a local chief or king, with his own warriors. The local farmers had little choice but to place themselves under the protection of these warlords, who took a share of the produce in what had largely become a cashless economy. Over time, this became formalised by custom and practice into the Feudal System, with each invasion or political upheaval bringing a change of landlord, if nothing else.

One early Saxon settlement has recently been identified from this chaotic period. Excavations in 1994, following the demolition of Tulse Hill School (in Upper Tulse Hill), revealed two Saxon buildings dated between 400 and 600 AD. There seems to have been a network of east-west tracks through the district, such as Acre Lane and Coldharbour Lane at the foot of the hill, between the marshy flood-plain of the Thames and the more thickly-wooded hills to the south. This site may have been an outpost where a few warriors could control east-west movement, while supporting themselves by farming.

Once the whole area was under unified control as part of Surrey (literally the Southern Region - of the Kingdom of Middlesex) this isolated outpost seems to have been abandoned and later ploughed over.

1.2 Saxon Hundred

The place-name Brixton is a simplified form of Brixistane, which meant the stone of Brixi or Beorhtsige, a Saxon lord who held several manors in the reign of King Edward the Confessor in the early 11th century. He must have erected a stone pillar as a boundary marker.

It was probably from that time that Brixistane became the name of the north-easternmost of the 14 hundreds or districts which made up the County of Surrey. Brixton Hundred embraced the modern boroughs of Wandsworth, Lambeth and Southwark, and continued to be used as a convenient term for the district into the 19th century.

But where was Brixi's Stone? In Saxon times the hundred court, or moot, would gather on some uninhabited moor or common - as neutral ground perhaps - to transact its business. Certainly there was no village or settlement identified as Brixton before about 1800, though what we now know as Brixton Hill was already being referred to as Bristow Causey or Brixton Causeway some 150 years earlier.

Recent research suggests the moot would have been near the top of Brixton Hill, within the triangle formed by its junctions with New Park Road (formerly Bleak Hall Lane) and Morrish Road (formerly Mill Lane). For centuries this was also the junction of the three parishes of Lambeth, Streatham and Clapham. Since parish boundaries would in turn have been based on the old manors or estates, this suggests that the place was long recognised as a boundary point. As for the hundred courts themselves, they were replaced in the reign of Edward III by Quarter Sessions, and eventually County Courts, so the hundred boundaries gradually lost their significance.

1.3 Manors & Estates

Our earliest detailed source for local history is Domesday Book, the great survey carried out for William the Conqueror in 1086. The Surrey chapter of Domesday Book names only 4 manors within the present boundaries of Lambeth - Clapham, Kennington, Lambeth and Streatham, although there are 2 entries for Lambeth:

The manor of St.Mary's called Lambeth, is described as land of Lambeth Church and included 42 households, with farmland for 12 ploughs, the whole valued at £11 for tax purposes. While the other manors correspond roughly to the modern districts, the lands of this Lambeth Manor extended south in an irregular strip from the riverside well into present-day Norwood.

The Count of Mortain also held an estate called Lambeth, with 18 households and land for 6 ploughs, valued at only £4. This estate is described in subsequent records as South Lambeth Manor.

Each manor had its own court and customary laws, to deal with disputes, grievances, minor offences or failure to perform feudal duties. Through his steward or bailiff, the owner or "Lord of the Manor" might supervise the farming of the land, keep accounts of rent, debts, stock and crops, and authorise improvements and repairs. Over the centuries, manor boundaries fluctuated due to bequests, dowries, leases and even gambling losses.

As more land was brought into cultivation and the woodlands were pushed back towards Norwood (literally the North Woods), additional manors or estates were established by sub-division of the original manors. Where a manor had been hived off or sub-let from an older manor, the original Lord of the Manor often retained control of the manorial court or rights for the newer estate.

At the end of the 13th century, the Manor of South Lambeth passed to the King, Edward III, and shortly afterwards was divided into the two separate manors of Vauxhall and Stockwell. Vauxhall was granted to the Dean and Chapter of Canterbury Cathedral to maintain a memorial chapel (or chantry) to Edward's son, the Black Prince (d.1376). Most of this Manor of Vauxhall lay north of the present Lansdowne Way, extending from Clapham Road to just west of Wandsworth Road, but also included some detached lands in Streatham and Mitcham.

The new Manor of Stockwell then included not only the small district now known by that name, but most of the western side of Brixton.

Its eastern boundary ran down Stockwell Park Road, Brixton Road and Brixton Hill, while the western boundary ran south from Clapham Road,

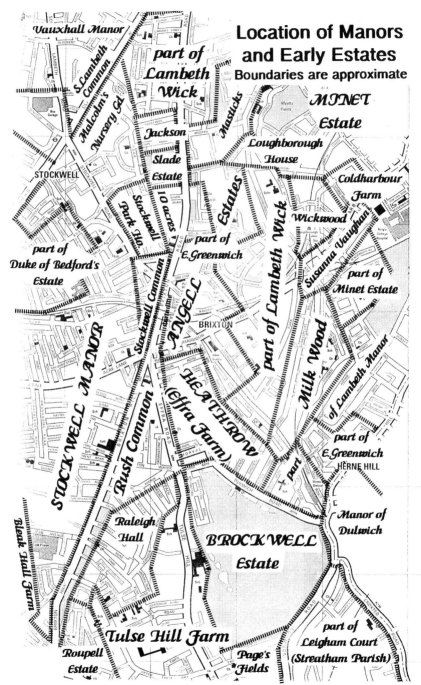

Location of Manors and Early Estates
Boundaries are approximate

Vauxhall Manor

part of Lambeth Wick

MINET Estate

S. Lambeth Common

Malcolm's Nursery Gd

Hasticks

Jackson Slade Estate

Loughborough House

Coldharbour Farm

STOCKWELL

10 acres

Stockwell Park Ho.

part of E. Greenwich

Wickwood

Estates

Susanna Vaughan

part of Minet Estate

part of Duke of Bedford's Estate

ANGELL

Stockwell Common

BRIXTON

part of Lambeth Wick

STOCKWELL MANOR

HEATHROW (Effra Farm)

Rush Common

Milk Wood

of Lambeth Manor

part of E. Greenwich

HERNE HILL

Bleak Hall Farm

Raleigh Hall

BROCKWELL Estate

Manor of Dulwich

Tulse Hill Farm

Roupell Estate

Page's Fields

part of Leigham Court (Streatham Parish)

Manors and early 19th century estates – superimposed on a modern street plan. (Alan Piper/ Brixton Society Collection) along Bedford Road and Lyham Road, roughly a diamond shape overall.

There was also a Stockwell Wood, not where its name suggests, but on the south-western boundary, part of the area later known as Clapham Park. Between Brixton Hill and New Park Road lay Bush Leas or Boshell Wood, belonging to the Manor of Leigham in Streatham Parish. By the 16th century both woods were being coppiced at 12 years growth to provide items like scaffold poles and broom handles.

In 1197 the Archbishop of Canterbury acquired the Manor of Lambeth from the Prior and Convent of Rochester, in exchange for estates in North Kent. Lambeth Palace was subsequently built next to the old church as a residence for the Archbishops, conveniently close to the seat of royal power at Westminster. The Archbishops continued as Lords of Lambeth Manor until 1862, when Church lands were consolidated under the control of the Church Commissioners.

From the end of the 13th century, the Manor of "Lambeth Wick" was administered as a separate unit from the original manor, and from 1480 onwards it was let to various tenants for a money rent. Lambeth Wick consisted of 3 separate parcels of land, one lying across Brixton Road northwards of Mostyn Road, another centred on the eastern arm of Loughborough Road, and the last in the Loughborough Park area.

Between these lands and Camberwell lay the Manor of Milkwell, first recorded in 1291, and covering the Myatts Field area, Denmark Hill and Herne Hill. Another small manor or farm detached from the Manor of Lambeth was Heathrow or Knight's Farm, bounded by the present Dulwich Road, Effra Road and Coldharbour Lane. The earliest references to this estate date from the 16th century.

Until the middle of the 17th century, 2 areas of woodland, reserved to the Archbishop of Canterbury, lay between Milkwell and Lambeth Wick manors. Wickwood lay to the east of Loughborough Road, around what is now Loughborough Junction Station. Its name is commemorated in the Wickwood Tavern, a Victorian public house in Flaxman Road. Milkwood extended not just along the present Milkwood Road, but further west across the railway tracks to include the northern arm of Shakespeare Road.

The areas now known as Tulse Hill and Brockwell Park correspond roughly with the 3 small manors or estates of Bodley, Upgrove and Scarlettes, first identified in early 14th century documents. In 1384, as a result of various bequests, these lands were consolidated in the hands of St. Thomas' Hospital (then a monastic establishment in Southwark) and remained undivided until 1807. Changes of ownership over the centuries resulted in several parcels of land (at Tulse Hill, Herne Hill and on the east side of Brixton Road) becoming attached to the Manor of East Greenwich, the Lewisham estates of the Earls of Dartmouth.

This early pattern of estate boundaries, served by a few roads, formed the basis of the future development of the area, as individual landowners sought to exploit their estates, usually without reference to each other.

1.4 The Rural Landscape

The landscape in those times was very different from what we see today, when most natural features have been obscured by buildings and roads. Moving southwards from the River Thames, through Lambeth, it is at Brixton that the ground first begins to rise from a low-lying plain. The ground was often marshy in places, hence the name Rush Common or Rushy Green for the tract of common land extending through the centre of Brixton until 1810.

Herne Hill, Brockwell Park and Tulse Hill are the first of a series of low hills leading up to Norwood, which remained largely wooded into the early years of the 19th century. Out of the Norwood hills flowed the River Effra, round the east side of Peabody Hill, then westwards between Herne Hill and Brockwell Park, along the line of Dulwich Road, then northward around Brixton to join Brixton Road close by the modern police station, continuing alongside the road well beyond the present junction with Vassall Road, thence north-westward to join the Thames just upstream of the present Vauxhall Bridge.

Fed by numerous streams and ditches, the Effra would have been about 3 metres wide at Brixton, but the culverts or low bridges carrying the Brixton Road and Clapham Road across it meant it was of little use for boats. In 1664, Lord Loughborough, then resident at the old manor house of Lambeth Wick, obtained an Act of Parliament to make the river navigable, but died before he could put it into effect.

Just over a hundred years ago, a local newspaper published a fanciful account of Queen Elizabeth I having sailed up the Effra to visit Sir Walter Raleigh at Brixton Hill, but the truth is less romantic. Queen Elizabeth certainly came to Stockwell, to dine with Lord Montague at his Stockwell Manor House in 1587, and Lambeth Parish Council spent 3 shillings on preparations for the Royal visit.

As for Sir Walter, there is no evidence that he owned any property locally.

14

Loughborough House in use as a school, c.1825 – a sketch left by one of the pupils. (Lambeth Archives)

In fact at this time he lived in the Strand, in a house provided by the Queen, and he would probably have been in attendance anyway as he was then Captain of the Royal Guard.

In addition to the original Roman Roads, there was a limited network of winding country lanes, probably of Medieval origin, some of which still retain their old names: Acre Lane, (Brixton) Water Lane and Coldharbour Lane (also known as Camberwell Lane in some old sources).

The Back Lane ran along the western edge of Stockwell Manor from Clapham Road to the top of Brixton Hill (the present Bedford and Lyham Roads) while Love Lane (later Stockwell Lane) led east from Stockwell Green to the Old White Horse in Brixton Road, whence another lane continued on the present line of Loughborough Road.

Railton Road and Landor Road originated in the late 18th century as convenient footpaths across the fields.

The first attempts to improve the road network were made in the early 18th century. In 1717, an Act of Parliament appointed Turnpike Trustees to make and maintain good toll roads along the length of the two old Roman roads previously referred to. Then in 1724, another Act provided for a similar road along the line of the present South Lambeth Road and Stockwell Road.

Most of the old wayside inns have continued - at least in name - down to the present day. The Swan on Clapham Road can be traced back to about

1450, and was an important coaching inn 200 years ago, as was the White Horse on Brixton Hill. (This and its namesake in Brixton Road both appear on a route map of 1790.) Three public houses at Stockwell Green were active in the 18th century, of which the New Queen's Head (now Galleon's Bar) is still in the original building of 1786.

London's growing demand for timber meant that the local woodlands disappeared during the 17th century, leaving a landscape largely of open fields. After years of regular coppicing, Stockwell Wood was finally cleared about 1630 and its 50 acres formed the basis of Bleak Hall Farm. Bleak Hall itself stood more or less on the site of the present Richard Atkins School in New Park Road.

During the Civil War, Parliament seized the estates of the Archbishop of Canterbury and sold them off. Although the estates were returned to the new Archbishop at the Restoration, in the meantime both Milkwood and Wickwood had been cleared of trees for a quick profit.

There were also patches of waste or common land, of lesser quality, where the tenants of each manor could graze their animals or gather firewood.

The Old White Horse Inn, on the corner of the present Brixton Road and Loughborough Road, as depicted in the 1780s. (Lambeth Archives)

Rush Common, belonging to the Manor of Lambeth, lay along the east side of Brixton Hill, while Stockwell Common was on the west side of Brixton Road, bounded by what are now Stockwell Park Walk and Stockwell Avenue. The land between Stockwell Green and Stockwell Road also served as common land, in fact the village green for Stockwell.

Further north, South Lambeth Common lay between Clapham Road and South Lambeth Road.

This farming landscape was thinly populated. In 1598, the whole of Stockwell contained only 10 houses, mostly clustered around the Green. Lambeth "Dean", comprising the eastern half of Brixton plus the whole of present-day West Norwood, totalled only 21 households. Numbers had changed little since a much earlier tax record of 1331, which listed 17 householders in Stockwell and South Lambeth (probably Vauxhall) and 26 in Lambeth Dean.

1.5 Country Life on London's Fringe

By the 18th century, the economy of country districts like Brixton was changing due to the proximity of London, the largest city of the kingdom. More land was being devoted to market gardening, providing fresh fruit and vegetables for London's markets, helped by copious supplies of its "night soil". It was also important to provide hay for a city dependent on horse transport, and grazing for animals being herded towards London to supply it with meat.

With more building and tile kilns, both locally and in London, some of the land was given over to brickfields, using the local clay.

Corn was still grown for local needs, and Brixton Hill made a fine site for a windmill to grind it into flour. By 1799 one had been built at the summit, halfway along the north side of the present Morrish Road (previously Mill Lane) but it was not to last.

After the Napoleonic Wars, the Admiralty adapted it for use as a semaphore signal station, part of a chain linking London with Portsmouth. However it was soon abandoned in favour of a shorter route via Wimbledon, and the mill had gone by the middle of the 19th century, though the brief use is commemorated in the name of the Telegraph public house nearby in Brixton Hill.

Meanwhile in 1816, another miller, John Ashby, had built a brick tower mill a little lower down the slope, and this windmill survives to the present day (off Blenheim Gardens). By 1862, the surrounding area had become too

Brixton's surviving windmill in Blenheim Gardens, photographed in the early 1970s (Lambeth Council)

built-up for it to operate efficiently, but it was then used for storage and even returned to milling from 1902 to 1934 (but with steam, and then gas, power).

1.6 Country Houses

The most substantial houses in the district were originally the manor houses, with their farmyards and kitchen gardens giving a workaday look. From the middle of the 18th century, well-to-do people began to use the area as a convenient retreat from the bustle of London, so a number of large new houses were built along the main roads, and some of the old manor houses were rebuilt in contemporary taste.

Brockwell Hall (1811-13) is the one surviving example in Brixton's orbit of a true country house still within its own landscaped park. The original Brockwell Hall was sited at the foot of the hill, opposite Crocksted Lane (now Croxted Road) but was demolished after John Blades, a City glass merchant, bought the eastern half of the Tulse Hill estate in 1809-10 and then had the new Hall built on top of the hill.

On the north-east side of Brixton, the old manor house of Lambeth Wick stood at the bend of what is now Loughborough Road. It was occupied by Henry Hastings, first Baron Loughborough and Lord Lieutenant of Leicestershire, from 1660 to his death in 1666, and subsequently known as Loughborough House. In the latter half of the 18th century, the house was

Stockwell Park House stood on the corner of Stockwell Road and Stockwell Park Walk. Originally built for John Angell around 1705, it became a school in the 1820s and was demolished in 1882. Its grounds are now occupied by the Stockwell Park Estate. (Lambeth Archives)

Cold Harbour, as sketched in July 1804, when this house would have been fairly new. The original Coldharbour Farm lay between the present Loughborough Junction and Camberwell Green. (Lambeth Archives)

Raleigh House, Brixton Hill, as it appeared in the 1880s, shortly before its demolition. (Brixton Society collection)

used as a boys' school, which continued almost up to its demolition in 1854. The outline of its triangular grounds (about 10 acres) is perpetuated in the layout of Claribel and Evandale Roads.

The medieval Stockwell manor house stood in 4 acres of gardens on the north-east side of Stockwell Road, south of the present Sidney Road and Robsart Street; its existence is commemorated by Moat Place nearby. In 1580 Lord Montague, then owner of the manor, sold the old house and had a new one built on a site further south (bounded by Stockwell Road, Stockwell Park Walk and the present Catholic Church).

In the early 18th century, John Angell senior replaced this with another new house, later known as Stockwell Park House, which survived until 1882.

The original manor house was demolished in 1755 and replaced by a smaller Georgian building, which was used as a candle wax factory from 1770 and finally demolished in 1865 when Sidney Road was built.

The chapel of the original building was still standing in 1801, and reputedly was still being used as a smithy (off Broomgrove Road) in 1913.

CHAPTER 2 - A LEAFY SUBURB

2.1 A Refuge from the City

By the end of the 18th century, the name of Brixton had become more focussed on the length of the Turnpike Road between the tollgate at Kennington Common and the hilltop we now know as Streatham Hill. This route was punctuated by a few small hamlets and occasional coaching inns, but the present Brixton Town Centre was still waste land.

The local population had increased gradually during the 18th century, mostly as a result of well-to-do City merchants looking for a convenient retreat from the bustle of the City, while still being close enough to keep in touch with their business affairs. Daily travel into town was still only practicable for those who could afford their own carriage and horses.

At first, substantial houses were built fronting onto the few existing roads, initially around Stockwell, then spreading further south as demand grew. Only scattered examples of these houses survive to the present day, often much altered after some 200 years of use.

40-46 Stockwell Road, flanking the entrance to the YMCA, are the survivors of 8 pairs of houses built between 1781 and 1788. A little further south, 146-166 Stockwell Road formed a more modest terrace which still bears the inscription "Queen's Row 1787", though long since converted into shops. Along the south-east side of Clapham Road, several of the houses built between 1791 and 1810 can still be seen. The oldest surviving houses in Brixton Road, 309-313, were built in 1801-2 at a slight angle to the road, perhaps due to a bend in the River Effra which ran alongside the road in front of the houses.

The early years of the 19th century saw a rapid transition of the Brixton area from a rural economy to an upmarket residential suburb. Landowners enclosed their waste or Common land and began to turn their best-placed fields into building plots.

The first substantial development in what we would now call the centre of Brixton came in 1800. A long terrace called Brixton Place was erected on the east side of Brixton Road, between Coldharbour Lane and Beehive Place. The mews or service road running behind the houses later became Electric Lane and Beehive Place.

In 1802, the Manor of Stockwell was split into a number of smaller plots and auctioned off to separate owners. As a result, large houses and villas began to appear along Acre Lane and the west side of Brixton Hill. Several examples remain, but the oldest survivor is 46 Acre Lane, dating from 1808 and now part of Robert Runcie Court.

2.2 The First Churches

Until well into the 18th century, all the inhabitants of Stockwell and Brixton looked to St.Mary's, alongside Lambeth Palace, as their parish church. The old Stockwell Manor House had had its own chapel, as perhaps did others, but after the Reformation such private chapels were liable to attract suspicion of dissent or covert Catholicism.

As early as 1711, residents had petitioned for another church to be built in the parish. Sir John Thornycroft, as Lord of Stockwell Manor, offered 2 acres of Stockwell Common to the "Commissioners for building 50 new churches in London, Westminster and the Suburbs," but they failed to follow it up.

St.Andrew's Church, Landor Road: a modern view, showing the tower and east window added in 1867 to celebrate the centenary of its opening as the Stockwell Chapel. (Lambeth Archives)

Numbers 208-218 Brixton Road are typical of the terrace houses built along the turnpike roads out of London in the early 19th century. Photograph taken c.1972, just before the houses were included in a Conservation Area. (Lambeth Archives)

Effra Hall, in Effra Road, typical of early 19th century villas in the south of the area. Depicted in the 1850s, when in use as a private asylum for "nervous, epileptic and insane ladies". (Lambeth Archives)

With the population of the district continuing to increase, eventually in 1767, Stockwell Chapel was erected by voluntary subscriptions as a "chapel of ease" at the corner of StackYard Field, then part of the Duke of Bedford's estate. In 1867, a century after its foundation, the building was extended, given a Venetian tower and facade, and in 1868 consecrated as St.Andrew's. Its Georgian origins were further obscured by rendering over the original grey brick in the 1880s, and by the removal of the side galleries in 1924.

Nonconformists also felt the need for a local place of worship, and the Stockwell Congregational Church was built off Stockwell Green in 1798, as Stockwell New Chapel. It was extended and given a new stucco front in 1850, but in 1989 the congregation moved to a more modest building in Stockwell Road and the chapel became a mosque.

2.3 Setting the Stage for Growth

In 1806, the Archbishop of Canterbury obtained a private Act of Parliament to enclose all the waste or common lands in his Manor of Lambeth. In Brixton, this chiefly involved Rush Common, which lay on the east side of the Turnpike Road. This land was finally divided up between the Archbishop and his various tenants in 1810. The award provided for Effra Road and St.Matthew's Road to be laid out, and for straightening out the west end of Brixton Water Lane, nearest Brixton Hill. Significantly for later development, generous building lines were included in the Act, to maintain the suburban character of the area and prevent buildings crowding too close to the roads.

As previously mentioned, on the west side of Brixton Road, the old manor of Stockwell had effectively come to an end in 1802, leaving the small Stockwell Common around the Brixton end of Stockwell Road. This too was soon enclosed, in 1813.

From 1816, the opening of Vauxhall Bridge hastened the southward expansion of the built-up area from old Lambeth. Within the following 10 years, large terraced houses and detached villas sprang up along Brixton Road and began to reach up Brixton Hill.

In 1821, the original Inclosure Act was amended to provide a site for a church where Acre Lane and Coldharbour Lane crossed the Turnpike Road. The consecration of St.Matthew's Church in 1824 provided this new suburb with a natural focal point. With City churchyards already full to overflowing, St.Matthew's new churchyard filled up with burials very rapidly. This does not mean local mortality was particularly high, but many well-to-do families had recently moved to the area, and took the opportunity to secure a decent resting place for relatives. All the old gravestones have long since been removed to make a public garden, but two memorials remain. The Budd memorial was erected in 1825 atop the family vault. Regarded from the outset as an impressive piece of funerary architecture, its scale is now rather exaggerated by an exposed position at the northern apex of the garden.

2.4 Garden Suburbs

From the 1820s onwards, developers found it worthwhile to lay out new residential streets off the existing roads, and to replace the paddocks and market gardens with new houses. Henry Vassall, 3rd Baron Holland of Foxley, began developing the Lambeth Wick estate, which his family had leased from the Archbishop of Canterbury since 1701. Camberwell New Road had been laid out in 1818, providing a direct link to the recently-opened Vauxhall Bridge, so the northern portion of the estate now had valuable frontages to this road and the northern part of Brixton Road. North Brixton or Holland Town, as contemporary maps label it, centred on Vassall Road and Foxley Road, consisting of substantial terraces and villas in the rather plain taste of the time.

West of Brockwell Park, the isolated Tulse Hill estate was developed more gradually by Dr. Thomas Edwards, a legal writer, who had acquired the property through his wife, Mercy Cressingham. In 1814 a small strip of land was purchased to give access onto Brixton Hill, then two curving roads (Tulse Hill and Upper Tulse Hill) were laid out, and formally adopted as parish highways in 1822. The estate was divided into building plots, and restrictive covenants in the leases ensured that the new roads were to be lined with large houses, generally detached, with commerce excluded.

By 1843 there were some 125 houses on the estate, with a continuous line from the Brixton end to the top of Tulse Hill. Only isolated examples have survived, such as No.47 Tulse Hill (now The Landmark Centre) from 1824. Trinity Rise was cut through to Norwood Road about 1851, and individual houses were still being added on the estate up to c.1890.

Although the northern section of Stockwell Park Road had been laid out in 1832, house-building only got underway after William Cox of Kennington purchased the land in 1838. Surviving houses in this road and

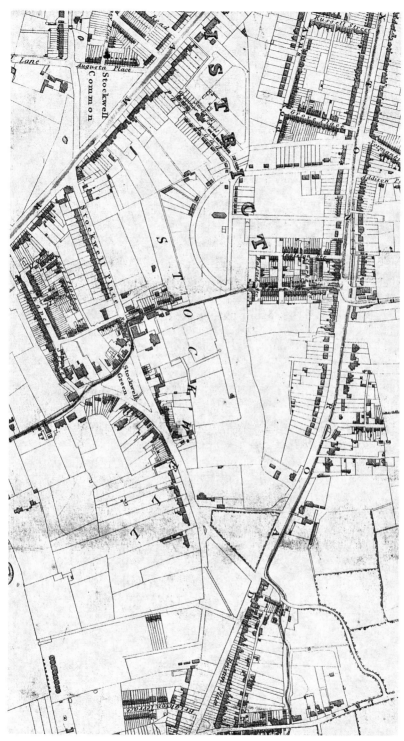

Stockwell Village and Brixton Road in 1841, with the first signs of building activity in the new suburb of Stockwell Park between them. (Lambeth Archives)

St. John's Church, Angell Town, seen across St. James's Crescent. Photographed c. 1956 when many substantial Victorian houses still stood around the church. (Lambeth Archives)

In the centre of Brixton Prison, the octagonal Governor's house of c. 1820 was intended to provide commanding views of the exercise yards and treadmills. The single-storey outbuilding was one of many additions later in the 19th century. (English Heritage)

Stockwell Park Crescent date from 1840 onwards, as do the similar Lorn Road and Groveway. The latter two streets were laid out on the gardens of a former house called Fir Grove.

These complementary estates consist of detached and semi-detached villas in a bolder style than the earlier terraces of Brixton and Clapham Roads. Several of the original houses on the south side of Lorn road are unusual for their time in having Gothic rather than Classical ornament.

Also from the 1840s, houses of a similar scale were being provided on the southern part of Lord Holland's Lambeth Wick Estate. This time there was more of an overall plan, provided by Henry Currey (later architect of St.Thomas' Hospital). He was responsible for the layout of St.James's Crescent, Barrington and Millbrook Roads (1843 onwards) and Loughborough Park (built 1844-57) though the detail of each group of houses seems to have been largely left to the builders. About half of Loughborough Park survives today, but only a few houses remain from the development further north.

Angell Town was laid out in the 1850s, with Wiltshire Road as its main axis and St.John's Church as the focal point. The land had previously been Stiles Farm, one of several small estates held by the Angell family since the late 17th century. The houses were generally in Italianate style, a mixture of detached, semi-detached and short terraces, all of substantial size. The grandest part of the development is Angell Terrace on Brixton Road. This was started in 1855 but the original builder went bankrupt and the terrace was not fully occupied until 1868. Most of the rest of the estate has disappeared in the past 50 years, but the remaining houses on the south side of St.John's Crescent are more typical of the whole.

2.5 The Developers

By the early 19th century, few of the landowners were themselves local residents, though sometimes their builders were. Even the Archbishops of Canterbury withdrew to Addiscombe when summer heat heightened the smells of the River Thames. Some had in any case more extensive estates elsewhere, such as the Angell family (at Crowhurst in Surrey). The Dukes of Bedford still owned 60,000 acres around the country, despite one Duke gambling away his Stockwell lands at cards.

Lord and Lady Holland are best known for hosting parties for the eminent people of the early 19th century at Holland House, a jacobean mansion whose grounds later became the suburb of Holland Park, Kensington. The

Edwards of Tulse Hill lived at Carshalton, at least in their later years.

Rather nearer were the Slade family of Walcott Place, Kennington Road, who speculated in developing sites on both sides of Brixton Road near the Old White Horse. Robert Slade's original holding forms the basis of the present Slade Gardens. His younger son Felix inherited the Brixton properties in 1858, and is mainly remembered for endowing the Slade School of Art at University College, London.

One of the local exceptions is Thomas Bailey, who lived at Bethel House, Brixton Hill (now the site of Corpus Christi Catholic Church). From 1802 he bought a couple of fields on the north side of Acre Lane and over the next 20 years erected a number of buildings, several of which survive, including 48-50 Acre Lane (The Cedars, completed 1819) currently used by Lambeth's Education Department.

His most notable building is Trinity Asylum (now Trinity Homes) which he built and endowed in 1822 for "pious aged females". Unusually, Bailey managed these almshouses himself until his death in 1828, when management passed to trustees.

In some cases, estates were developed by trustees to realise the assets of a deceased owner, such as Lord Thurlow, who had acquired much of Norwood and a little of Brixton before his death in 1806.

Some of his land south of Tulse Hill was bought between 1811 and 1818 by John Roupell, a successful scrap metal dealer of Blackfriars. His son Richard Palmer Roupell inherited his father's estates in 1835, and about 1840 he began development of the Roupell Park Estate, centred on Christchurch and Palace Roads. (Strictly speaking, most of this was in the Parish of Streatham, but Brixton Hill was regarded as extending much further southwards until the development of Streatham Hill in the 1930s - hence Brixton bus garage, so-called.)

By 1853, management of the estate, with its own brickworks, was being handled by R.P.Roupell's eldest but illegitimate son, William. On his father's death in 1856, he forged a will which gave him effective control of this and the other estates. The next year, his new-found wealth helped him get elected as an MP for Lambeth, but in 1862, having spent most of his money and fearing exposure, he fled to Spain. He returned voluntarily after a few months and was duly tried and given a life sentence. He eventually served 14 years and then returned to the family home, Aspen House on Brixton Hill (a site now occupied by the Stratstone Garage). William spent his remaining years quietly at Harvey Lodge, opposite Christ Church with which he remained closely involved.

2.6 Building a Community

Many estate owners helped establish churches on their land, thereby giving their new developments some appearance of community. To provide a site or contribute to the cost was probably motivated more by the potential for attracting discerning tenants, than by religious conviction, but at least provision kept up with the growing local population.

One of the first examples was St.Michael's, whose site was provided in 1839 by William Cox, in the course of laying out Stockwell Park. Similarly, Benedict Angell gave the site for St.John's Church in 1852, just as development of Angell Town was getting underway.

In 1867, Joshua Blackburn paid part of the cost of St.Jude's Church, Dulwich Road, probably with a view to eventually developing the rest of his Brockwell Hall estate.

The Clergy generally saw these new churches as the means to reclaim a growing urban population that was beginning to lose its traditional religious habits. Occasionally though there was opposition from existing churches who felt their market was being encroached upon. Thus in 1855, when Jonah Cressingham gave a site on his Tulse Hill Estate for Holy Trinity Church, there was vigorous opposition from the Vicars of St.Matthew's at Brixton, and St.Luke's, its sister church at Norwood. Both feared that their churches would lose members and support from what was then a very well-to-do area.

The churches were active in meeting the need for schools for a growing number of children. One of the first local day schools was opened in 1818 as the Stockwell and Brixton Auxiliary Parochial School. It still continues on the same site (in modern buildings) as St.Andrew's Primary School, Lingham Street.

St.Matthew's Church similarly founded a school in 1828. Its premises in St.Matthew's Road were rebuilt in 1871, but demolished after heavy damage in the Second World War. St.Paul's Church, Herne Hill, started a school in what is now Railton Road in 1834, taken under the wing of the new St.Jude's Church in 1869. St.John's School was established in Canterbury Road (now Crescent) in 1853. Both these buildings survive, somewhat altered, in other uses.

Nonconformist churches were equally keen to provide schools, theirs being organised under the "British Schools" system, while those of the Church of England were "National Schools". The Stockwell Congregational Chapel opened its school at 1 Stockwell Green in June 1848. Free education was yet

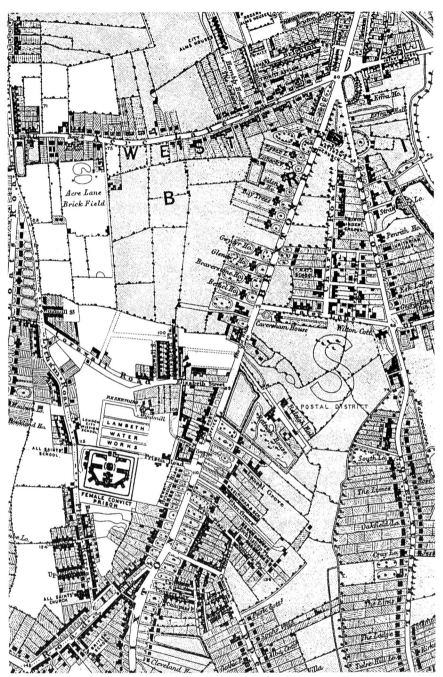

Brixton Hill: extract from Stanford's map of 1862, showing large houses along the main roads. Most of the land behind them was then still open fields, but the arrival of railways and tram services would soon change that. (Brixton Society collection)

to come - fees were 6d. a week for seniors, 3d. a week for younger children, with slates and copybooks bought by parents. As the Stockwell Educational Institute, the building also accommodated evening classes for adults.

There had long been private schools in the area, but they catered for a more well-to-do class. Any large house might be used as an "academy", often with just one master (perhaps assisted by his wife) or one mistress or dame. In the 1780s there was one such academy at Love Lane, Stockwell, and another near the Green Man at Coldharbour (now Loughborough Junction).

Some schools provided accommodation and augmented the basic teaching with special subjects from visiting teachers for additional payment. Loughborough House was being used in this way as a "superior academy for young gentlemen" by the late 18th century, and had 30 resident pupils at the 1841 Census. Stockwell Park House was also used as a school from the 1820s, until its demolition in 1882. James Hine opened an academy for gentlemen boarders at Brixton Lodge in 1824, which continued until 1880 when most of the grounds were sold off to build Tunstall Road.

There were also a number of residential institutions established by charities for orphans or foundlings. St.Ann's Asylum (founded in the City in 1702) was established at the very top of Brixton Hill in 1830 after a move from Peckham. It eventually housed nearly 400 boys and girls, but moved on again to Redhill in 1884, the site now being occupied by Pullman Court, Streatham Hill.

The Girls Industrial Home, founded around 1860 at 57 Stockwell Road, was one of several charitable establishments set up to train girls for domestic service. It continued until 1907. The City of London Freemen's Orphan School opened in Ferndale Road in March 1854, accommodating 65 boys and 35 girls. Enlarged to take 150 children in 1863, it moved to Ashtead Park, Surrey in 1926, and the site was next used for flats and a sports club for the City of London Police.

The Stockwell Orphanage was established in 1867 by Charles Spurgeon, minister of the Metropolitan Tabernacle at the Elephant and Castle. Initially intended as a home for fatherless boys, it was extended in 1880 to accommodate orphaned girls too, eventually housing 500 children between the ages of 6 and 10. Later known as Spurgeon's Homes, the orphanage was evacuated to Reigate at the outbreak of the Second World War, and never returned to Stockwell. The site is now occupied by Stockwell Park Secondary School.

2.7 The House of Correction

In 1818, the Justices of the Peace for Surrey bought about 5 acres of what had latterly been the Nine Acres Field of Stockwell Manor, and in 1819 work started on building a new prison. Once the wall and gatehouse were complete, 25 prisoners were sent to help in the work, but 3 escaped in 1820 and the governor was dismissed. As first completed, the prison consisted of an octagonal house for the governor in the centre, and 6 cell blocks arranged in a crescent, totalling 149 single and 12 double cells. In 1836 the site was extended westwards to the Back Lane (now Lyham Road) after buying a strip of land from the Lambeth Waterworks Company.

Following the completion of a large new "House of Correction" at Wandsworth, the Surrey Justices sold Brixton Prison in 1852 to William Tite, architect of West Norwood Cemetery, who intended to demolish it and sell the reclaimed building materials. In the meantime, Lord Palmerston had been appointed Home Secretary and proposed to abolish transportation to the colonies, requiring more prison accommodation. So in February 1853, Tite was able to sell the old prison to the government for a substantial profit. It was then enlarged and remodelled to accommodate 700 women convicts.

It later became a military prison, but returned to civilian use before the end of the 19th century. In 1897, John Lewis, founder of the John Lewis Partnership, spent 3 weeks in Brixton Prison after defying a court injunction against extending his Oxford Street store into Cavendish Square.

2.8 Early Industry

Industry failed to make much impact on the area, probably due to local landowners' anxiety to maintain the prestige (and rents) of their new suburban estates, though some isolated works and utilities gained a foothold. The pattern might have been very different if the Surrey Canal had crossed Brixton as projected in 1801, linking Mitcham with the Thames at Deptford. The entrance lock from the Thames opened in 1807 but the Grand Surrey Canal Company was consistently short of money to advance the works, and the canal stopped just short of Camberwell Road, in what is now Burgess Park.

Due probably to the ready availability of water from wells, there were two breweries at Stockwell Green by the 1860s. On the north side of the Green stood the oldest, latterly known as Hammerton's. An auction notice of the

1830s claimed it had been established more than 50 years, though an inscription displayed in later years of "established 1730" has never been substantiated. This brewery was eventually replaced by a beer-bottling plant, built in 1964-68, though an 1888 pub on the opposite side of Lingham Street is still called "The Brewery Tap".

Waltham Brothers' brewery stood at the southern end of the Green, on the corner of Combermere Road. By 1913 it had been taken over by the Lambeth Borough Council as a cleansing depot, though little use was made of the buildings after 1964. In 1995 a painted sign for "Waltham Brothers Half Guinea Ale" was still legible on a gable end of the old buildings, which remained in outline unchanged from a photograph taken before 1876.

As more houses were built, wells alone could no longer provide enough water and piped supplies were gradually introduced to the district. The early

Hammerton's Stockwell Brewery, corner of Stockwell Green and Lingham Street, photographed shortly before its demolition c.1964. The buildings seen here date from c.1870, but the brewery had been operating since at least the 1780s. (Lambeth Archives)

19th century was a time of competing water companies, and though the South London Water Works Company negotiated with John Roupell in the 1820s, it was the Lambeth Water Works Co. which actually secured a site of 16 acres on Brixton Hill in 1832.

The first two reservoirs were built there in 1834-35, and water was pumped by steam engine from the Thames at Belvedere Wharf, to be distributed to customers down the hill by gravity. After 1840, rough sand filters were added, which was just as well given the increasing pollution of the Thames in Central London, and the cholera epidemics which swept the riverside districts in the 1840s. From 1852, the Belvedere Wharf intake closed and water was pumped to the Brixton works from much higher up the river at Ditton. The reservoirs were covered over in 1855, and from 1904 the company and its works became integrated into the London-wide network of the Metropolitan Water Board. Little now survives from the early days, following a major remodelling of the works completed in 1933, and replacement of earlier machinery by electrical pumps in 1974.

Drainage also began to receive some attention. In 1847, the local Commissioners for Sewers culverted the River Effra, which ran along the east side of Brixton Road. It flooded in stormy weather, and was carrying away the waste products of a growing number of people, so the immediate problem was solved by putting it underground.

The Metropolitan Board of Works was established in 1855 to tackle issues like drainage on a London-wide basis. This involved massive new sewers running from west to east, across the line of the existing streams draining to the Thames. In 1859, work started on the Southern High Level Sewer, running from Clapham, through Brixton and Camberwell to a pumping station at Deptford. Roads were dug up to a depth and width of some 5 metres, to allow the construction of a brick pipe averaging 3 metres in diameter.

CHAPTER 3 - THE RAILWAY BOOM

3.1 The Railways Arrive

The railways were a little late in coming to this part of Lambeth, but for ten years there was hectic construction activity as first one line, then another, crossed the Brixton area. The London Chatham & Dover Railway, seeking direct access from East Kent to Central London, ran the first line along the eastern fringes of Brixton in 1862, approaching from Penge via Herne Hill to Farringdon Street in the City. This was followed immediately by another line, completed the next year, branching off at Herne Hill to cross Brixton Road on its way to the new Victoria Station.

Initially the different lines crossing South London represented the ambitions of competing railway companies, but in the course of the 1860s Parliament began to impose some co-ordination, so that a number of lines were eventually shared. Thus a line linking Victoria and London Bridge was built as a joint effort by the London Chatham & Dover and their erstwhile rivals, the London Brighton and South Coast. Most of this line was carried across low-lying ground on viaducts of brick arches, and in 1864, 19 newly-built arches collapsed at Brixton when the centering was removed. High bridges were also required to carry this new "South London Line" over the existing L.C.& D. lines at Brixton and at Loughborough Junction.

This was all completed in 1867, but 1872 saw a further burst of construction around Loughborough Junction, when the Crystal Palace & South London Junction Railway demolished some recent houses in Flaxman Road, to add a spur linking to their Peckham line. Further south, the L.C.& D. built another line in 1869 from Herne Hill to Tulse Hill station, linking up with the Peckham to Streatham line already being built by the London, Brighton & South Coast.

3.2 Terraces & Artisans' Dwellings

In order to obtain Parliamentary approval, the railway companies were obliged to provide cheap early morning workmen's fares, and these, combined with the ease of travel offered by the new railways, enabled workers to live in one district and work in another. Workers were no longer tied to overcrowded lodgings within walking distance of Central London. The result was the rapid development around the new railway stations of new suburbs of terraced housing for the skilled working classes.

Simple 2-storey terraces like these were already beginning to branch off the main roads even before the railways arrived. Here in Blenheim Gardens, off Brixton Hill, the entrance to a small Baptist Chapel adds variety. Most of this area was rebuilt in 1968-72 but a few cottages survive along Lyham Road. (Lambeth Archives)

At first much of the new housing continued to include basements and attics, in an attempt to attract middle class tenants who might still have a couple of servants living in. However, by the end of the 1870s the main types being built were 2 or 3 storey houses with the principal rooms at ground level, intended for "artisans", the skilled working class family. Plans were more compact than previously, 3 or 4 rooms deep on a frontage of less than 5 metres. Architects were rarely involved, local builders usually being engaged to build up to 10 houses at a time to "pattern book" designs.

If the first houses let successfully, the developer would repeat the process until all his land had been covered with houses. By this stage, few developers concerned themselves with the sort of estate planning attempted in earlier years, and adjoining fields might be laid out with little co-ordination as to street pattern. Some of the consequences can be seen today in roads like Railton Road left with a kink where two different developments met.

Two larger estates off Railton Road show contrasting patterns of development. The south-eastern half of the former Effra Farm was acquired by the Westminster Freehold Land Society in 1855. Their intention was to

Somerleyton Road was one of many streets built around 1870, following the arrival of suburban railway services. Larger houses like these were soon being shared or used as boarding houses. This was one of the main areas of West Indian settlement in the 1950s, and was demolished in 1967-68, shortly after the photograph was taken. (Greater London Record Office)

39

divide the land into plots for individual houses, whose purchasers would thereby qualify as voters. Chaucer, Spenser, Shakespeare and Milton Roads were laid out, but few houses had been built before the opening of Herne Hill Station in 1862. In 1867 the Government abolished the property qualification for voters, and most of the plots were developed on a piecemeal basis, with 2, 3 or 4 small houses on each. The eventual result was a great variety of "pattern book" houses spanning the period 1855 to 1885.

Further north, a consortium of Scottish developers followed a more conventional pattern for another large parcel of Effra Farm, covered with houses between 1873 and 1879. In contrast to the "Poets" Roads, the houses and shops show a consistent style across the "Effra Hall Estate". Houses ranged from grand 5-storey terraces on Effra Road itself, down through subtle gradations of size and ornament to 2-storey cottages at the southern extremity in Barnwell Road.

There was strong demand during the 1870s, not just from families moving outwards from older areas like Kennington, but also from people flocking to London from country districts in search of jobs, for agriculture was in long-term decline. In some neighbourhoods therefore, many of the new houses were soon being shared by families.

For example a 3-storey house in Saltoun Road (built in 1874) accommodated a separate household on each floor at the time of the 1881 Census. On the ground floor were an ageing grocer's assistant, his wife and a young lodger. The first floor was occupied by a milk carrier, his wife and 3 children (2 being in their teens) while the top floor was taken by an unmarried mother and her baby. The Census gave each person's parish of birth, and in this example the grocer's assistant and the milk carrier had recently brought their families to London from the depths of Norfolk and Wiltshire respectively.

3.3 Tracing Victorian Street Names

In the early Victorian period, Royal or aristocratic references were often used to give a new development a suitably up-market sound. Rustic place-names were replaced by the blandly suburban: thus, the eastern half of Brixton Water Lane became Dulwich Road. Some names became rather overworked as at this time any house numbering ran within the individual terrace or block, rather than for the street as a whole. Larger detached houses retained their individual names - which might even change with a

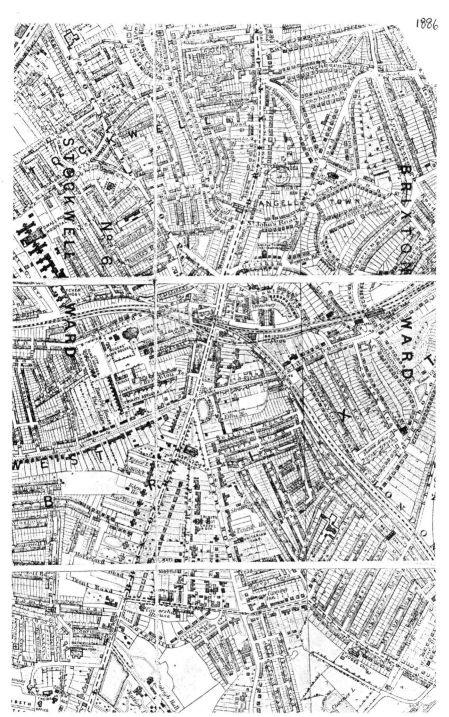

Central Brixton in 1886, with the street pattern almost complete.
(Brixton Society collection)

Brixton's first Fire Station was built in Ferndale Road in the 1870s, shortly before the Bon Marche department store was put up on the opposite side of the road. The building still survives, now adapted as offices. (Greater London Record Office)

Acre Lane on a postcard of 1903, looking towards Brixton from near Ballater Road. The houses on the right still survive but lost most of their front gardens – and the trees – when the road was widened about 10 years later. (Brixton Society collection)

change of owner! Thus the present 186-220 Brixton Road originally comprised 1-4 Grove Place and then in turn, Grove House, Elm House, 1-4 Fir Grove Place, Fir Grove House, and only then 7-13 Grove Place.

As a result of the introduction of the Penny Post in 1840, and then the dramatic increase in the number of houses in London and its suburbs, naming and numbering of streets was gradually put on a more rational basis. Most residential streets were still named by the developers who laid them out. They might commemorate their home links or family members, or occasionally a topical reference, such as Rhodesia Road, Stockwell, which must date from the 1890s. By the end of the 19th century, the London County Council was regulating street names and starting to eliminate duplication, with one eye on the need to send its fire brigade to the right address. Then during the First World War, there was a widespread revulsion against names of German origin, resulting in more changes.

In consequence, many of the addresses of a hundred years ago have been changed, sometimes more than once. Although there has often been a desire to retain historical links when naming new streets or buildings, the location may not necessarily coincide with the original associations. For example, Minet Road is not on the old Minet Estate at all, but within Lord Holland's Lambeth Wick Estate, and indeed was previously called Holland Road.

3.4 Omnibus & Tram

Omnibuses (later shortened to buses) served Brixton from the 1830s. Early in the field were the Balls family, who lived in 2 houses on the east side of Brixton Hill. Originally they were "jobmasters" who provided horses and carriages for hire, but they soon went into the omnibus business. In the early days, London omnibus operators were licensed by the Board of Stamps, and their official list for 1838-39 mentions 4 members of the Balls family who were authorised to run buses on different routes between Brixton Hill and the City or West End. Their brightly-painted single-decker buses (usually green) were drawn by 2 horses with one driver. Most of the Balls buses had "Brixton" and the name of their Central London termini painted on them, but some were named "Paragon". Those were Balls buses which originally ran to the "Crown and Sceptre" tavern at the top of Brixton Hill, near the home of a Mr Paragon who had invented a patent umbrella frame named after him.

To begin with, fares were not cheap, reflecting the limited number of seats, the cost of horses' fodder, and of course the toll charges on the

Turnpike Roads. It might be as much as 9d. from Brixton Hill to the City, though fares got lower towards the end of the century, with larger buses and more competition.

In the 1850s came the "knifeboard" omnibus with an open upper deck reached by stairs at the rear. These might carry up to 12 people inside and 15 on top - and fares might be lower for those sitting outside. A further boost came with the abolition of tolls and the removal of the Kennington Tollgate in 1865.

Like many English institutions, the omnibus was invented in Paris, and it was actually the French who started the London General Omnibus Company in 1856. The French owners wanted to buy out all the other bus concerns in London, but their London managers were opposed to acquiring South London enterprises like Thomas Tilling's and the Balls' buses. So these two firms, which then owned 210 buses between them, stayed independent and even worked in co-operation with LGOC to some extent.

The first tram services were introduced to Brixton in May 1870, initially running from the Horns Tavern at Kennington and along Brixton Road to its junction with Stockwell Road. Each tram was pulled by 2 horses but rails presented less friction than the roads of the time so passenger capacity far exceeded the horse buses - 22 people inside and 24 more on the open top deck. The normal fare was a penny a mile, but as with the railways, Parliament required special early morning and evening services for workmen at reduced fares, in this case a halfpenny a mile.

By the end of 1870, the service ran from the Lambeth end of Westminster Bridge to St.Matthew's Church at Brixton, extended the following year up Brixton Hill as far as its junction with Brixton Water Lane. In the meantime, another service ran along Clapham Road, initially to the Swan at Stockwell, also extended in 1871 to the Plough at Clapham. During the 1880s, additional tracks for horse trams were laid along Stockwell Road, Gresham Road and Coldharbour Lane to Camberwell Green, from Loughborough Junction via Milkwood Road and Norwood Road to Tulse Hill and West Norwood, and along South Lambeth Road to link Stockwell with Vauxhall Station.

Brixton Hill was really too steep for two horses to pull a loaded tram, and in December 1892 the London Tramways Co. started a cable-driven service. Horses were detached from southbound trams at Kennington, and a small tractor or "gripper-car" substituted. This gripped a moving cable set into a conduit between the tracks, a continuous loop attached to steam-driven winding gear at the very top of Brixton Hill. Attached to this cable, trams could move up (or down) the hill at a steady 8 mph, all the way to Telford Avenue. The service was extended on to the Streatham Tate Library by the end of 1895, and remained in use until electrification in 1904.

3.5 Church & Chapel

While most developers tended to work with the Established Church, William Higgs (senior) was a keen supporter of the eminent Baptist preacher, Charles Haddon Spurgeon. In 1883 Higgs provided a site and a design for a chapel in Solon Road, but died before the plans could be put into effect. His family met the building cost in his memory, and Spurgeon himself laid the foundation stone of the Kenyon Baptist Chapel in November 1884.

In general though, the other denominations provided their churches and chapels through their own efforts, sometimes starting on quite a modest basis. As Brixton's population increased rapidly during the 1870s, some congregations - such as Railton Methodist Church - made use of prefabricated corrugated iron chapels until permanent buildings could be provided. The largest example was Torrey & Alexander's temporary mission church on what became the site of Lambeth Town Hall. Just one of these "tin" chapels still survives in religious use, in Hetherington Road, off Acre Lane.

The Churches played a very active role in social improvement and welfare, often providing more substantial help for their members than was then available from state or local authority sources. Some saw this as a social duty, others more as a way of swelling their congregation. In building terms, this was reflected by the construction of many church halls, sunday schools and mission churches in the last quarter of the 19th century. These were sometimes sited away from the original church in an attempt to meet the needs of a poorer part of the parish. Thus in 1888, St.Matthew's was using a former shop at 8 Mayall Road as mission rooms, shortly to be superseded by its church hall in Talma Road, just the other side of Railton Road.

3.6 The Victorians at Leisure

There had long been wayside inns, but in Victorian times, the Public House became a more distinctive feature in the new residential areas.

They were generally a little larger than the surrounding houses and shops, with bolder ornament outside and richer decoration inside.

Towards the end of the century, some were rebuilt on an even grander scale, such as the "George Canning" (now Hobgoblins, Brixton Water Lane) and the "Loughborough Hotel" (Loughborough Road).

There were also "beer houses", generally smaller, which sold ale but not spirits. Changes in licensing laws before and during the First World War meant that most of them went back to being shops or ordinary houses, such as 233 Railton Road, once the "Brittania".

In the last quarter of the 19th century, the north-east side of Brixton attracted a lot of music hall performers. By this time, some of the larger houses were being given over to use as boarding houses, and performers could get back to their lodgings from the West End theatres using the late-night tram service.

Dan Leno was one of the leading music hall comedians from the 1880s until his death (aged only 44) in 1904. He lived at 56 Akerman Road from 1898 to 1901, and the house now bears a blue plaque.

Prior to the First World War, Fred Karno's "Fun Factory" was at 40 Southwell Road, near Loughborough Junction. This was the base for rehearsals and scenery painting, from which his troupe of performers would set out on tour. Charlie Chaplin and Stan Laurel worked for him early in their careers, before finding greater fame in films.

In the early years of the 20th century, we find other artistes living further up Brixton Hill, a few more stops on the tram service. Will Fyfe lived in Tulse Hill. Naughton and Gold (later to be members of the Crazy Gang) lived in Raleigh Gardens. The comedian Max Wall was born in Brixton of theatrical parents in 1908. The music hall singer Kate Carney lived at 243 Brixton Hill, on the corner of Christchurch Road, with her husband, George Barclay, a leading theatrical agent.

3.7 *Public Parks & Gardens*

With the countryside being pushed ever further away by the pace of new building, local residents were increasingly anxious to safeguard some open spaces for public recreation. Most of the traditional Common land had already been enclosed, but at Stockwell the old village green survived into the 1870s. There was a great outcry in 1876 when a developer began building on Stockwell Green, but although objectors took the case to court, they were unable to prove any continuing rights of common or access. As a result the whole site was soon filled with houses and shops, leaving just one

PARK FOR BRIXTON

A GRAND

DEMONSTRATION

WILL BE HELD IN

RALEIGH HOUSE GROUNDS

BY THOSE IN FAVOUR OF THE

PUBLIC PARK,

ON

SATURDAY, OCTOBER 1st, 1887,

AT FOUR O'CLOCK P.M.

THE

MARQUIS OF CARMARTHEN, M.P.

WILL PRESIDE,

Supported by several prominent Local Gentlemen,

(SEE LIST OF COMMITTEE.)

All who are in favour of the movement are earnestly requested to attend.

LADIES ARE ALSO INVITED.

JOHN. FENTON, "EAGLE PRINTING WORKS," 304, BRIXTON ROAD.

A Park for Brixton – 1887 campaign poster for the grounds of the old Raleigh House to be used as a public park. While Brixton's MP was supporting this cause, Norwood's MP, Thomas Bristow, was soon championing the larger grounds of nearby Brockwell Hall, eventually opened as Brockwell Park. (Lambeth Archives).

path as an alleyway (now Stockwell Green Court).

Local concerns were also supported by three new campaigning bodies, the Commons Preservation Society (founded 1865), the Kyrle Society (founded by Octavia Hill in 1877) and the Metropolitan Public Gardens Association (1882). In 1887 the Lambeth Vestry was persuaded to begin negotiations to purchase the grounds of Raleigh House, Brixton Hill, as a public park for the Brixton area. However in the following year, Joshua Blackburn III inherited the larger Brockwell Hall estate, which was soon put on the market for development. Local opinion soon switched from the proposed Raleigh Park to the potential Brockwell Park, and the authorities were eventually persuaded to divert the funds and effort to the larger site.

The first 78 acres of Brockwell Park were bought by the London County Council in 1891, with contributions from the Vestries of Lambeth, Camberwell and Newington, the Church Commissioners, the Charity Commissioners and the local campaigning committee. Even Mr Blackburn himself was persuaded to contribute £2,000.

The formal opening on 6th June 1892 was overshadowed by the collapse of the Norwood MP, Thomas Bristowe, from a heart attack. He had played a leading part in the acquisition of the Park, chairing the campaign committee. His work was soon continued by a "Brockwell Park Extension Committee" to acquire the remainder of the estate, and access from the Brixton direction, via Arlingford Road, was opened in 1896. The formation of Brockwell Park as we know it today was a piecemeal process, only completed in 1939 when the LCC opened a new access onto Tulse Hill, with a pedestrian link through their new housing estate to the Brixton Hill area once intended for Raleigh Park.

William Minet was one of the few landlords to see that providing amenities of this kind made the rest of his estate more attractive in the long term (and so helped keep up rents). He donated the site for Myatt's Fields Park to the London County Council. It was laid out by the Metropolitan Public Gardens Association and opened in April 1889.

CHAPTER 4 -
THE RISE OF THE SHOPPING CENTRE

4.1 Population Pressure & Market Forces

Brixton has had a relatively short lifespan as a shopping centre: unlike other London centres, it did not grow out of an established village or market town. During the first half of the 19th century, large houses for City merchants and professional people had spread along the main roads, and new suburban developments were laid out off the existing roads. There were also groups of humbler cottages for servants and small tradesmen, but in the 1850s the overall appearance of Brixton's "Town Centre" must have been very much like Dulwich Village today.

When the railways came to Brixton in the 1860s, they opened up the district to humbler classes, clerks and skilled workers, who no longer needed to live close to their work in Central London, but could now travel in each morning from new terraced houses on the edge of town. The houses built for these new residents were more closely packed than before, but still

Brixton Road seen from the corner of Acre Lane, at Christmas 1885, before most of the shopping development got under way. On the opposite corner, a cabmen's shelter beneath the sign of the Prince of Wales public house, with a waiting horse bus. The railway bridges are just visible in the distance on the left. (Lambeth Archives)

415-417 Brixton Road: this shop on the corner of Atlantic Road was built for Francis' Exchange Stores, then later taken over by Woolworth's, before their new store was built further south c.1936. (Lambeth Archives)

Electric Avenue, built in 1888 with glazed canopies over both sides of the shopping street. Viewed from Brixton Road in 1904. (Brixton Society collection)

substantial, while for the time being, the "carriage trade" remained in areas like Brixton Hill, further from the railway lines.

So we see during the 1860s and 1870s a great increase in the number of people living around Brixton, and thus a greater local demand for shopping and services. Most of this would have been met from small shops, market stalls and itinerant traders. The first purpose-built shops in the Centre were put up close to the railway station in Atlantic Road and Coldharbour Lane, immediately after the first railway viaducts were completed.

In those days before planning control, most landlords were happy for their houses to be turned over to shops, as they could command higher rents. As demand increased, some of the larger houses fell victim to this trend. The original porch and bay window might give way to a new shopfront, or a shop might even be built out over the front garden.

In Brixton Road, south of the new railway, the front gardens were exceptionally long due to the building lines created by the Rush Common Inclosure Act. Commercially, this was a very attractive and central location, so there was a gradual intensification of use, from market stalls through hoardings, shelters and small buildings towards permanent shops. By 1888, J.W.Clark's Exchange Stores had extended over the former front gardens of 415 & 417 Brixton Road, at the corner of Atlantic Road. On the other side of Brixton Road, a complete terrace of shops was erected in the 1880s in front of the original houses, one of which still stands behind Morleys in what is now Bernays Grove.

4.2 The Victorian Shopkeeper

It is important to recognise that shopping has changed in many ways since Victorian times. Most households would need to make some purchases every day, as there were no refrigerators or freezers to keep food fresh. Cookery was more labour-intensive, with preserved or mass-produced foods only coming into use gradually in the course of the 19th century. The larger villas might be more self-sufficient, with their own kitchen garden and orchard, perhaps even an ice-house, and with local tradesmen delivering on a regular basis. Among the smaller cottages there would still be people keeping chickens in the backyard or growing some of their own vegetables. Poorer folk often depended on buying whatever they could find at the end of the day, when traders sold off their remaining produce cheaply because it would not keep.

A much wider range of goods would be sold from door to door, and there was still a great deal of small-scale local production and repair. Any significant road which might bring passing trade was lined with a high proportion of shops, such as Railton Road, Landor Road and Acre Lane. Most newly-built neighbourhoods were generously provided with local shopping parades and corner shops. Just a few of the more select residential estates (particularly Tulse Hill and the Minet Estate) enforced restrictive covenants and banished any visible "trade" to their edges.

The big shop window became the dominant feature of every shop in Victorian times, but internally the arrangement was much the same as any other small house, with the front room being used for business while the rest of the space was occupied by the shopkeeper's household. When a business became more successful, the owner might move out to a larger house, perhaps up the hill like David Greig in Brixton Hill. Mr Axtens of Quin & Axtens moved even further on, to Leigham Court Road, Streatham, but he left a nephew living in Gresham Road near the shop, as his Assistant Manager. Some of the space vacated this way might be used to enlarge the sales area or for stock-holding, but some of the young shop assistants would probably still be housed on the upper floors.

Brixton Road seen from the Town Hall Tower, c.1913, with shops covering the former Stockwell Common. Note the Empress Theatre in its original form on the far left of the picture. (Lambeth Archives)

Electric Avenue, decorated for Christmas shopping c.1911. (Linskey Collection)

4.3 The Big Stores Arrive

In 1876, James Smith, having won £48,000 on the horses, decided to put his money into a store. On the site of a nursery garden, he built the Bon Marche, which opened in 1877 as Britain's first purpose-built department store, patterned after its Paris namesake. By 1888, it employed over 400 people. Although Mr Smith went bankrupt in 1892, a new partnership took over and enlarged the store in that year. By that time, the store was the focal point of a flourishing shopping centre.

Other major stores came up the hard way, starting as single shops and expanding into neighbouring premises until they might control a whole shopping parade, such as Quin & Axtens, next to Bon Marche, or Morley & Lanceley (opposite the present Tube station).

Morley's, as they became, had a disastrous fire in 1910, but then rebuilt their premises on a larger scale, filling the whole site.

Other traders, such as David Greig, chose to expand by opening new branches further afield, rather than add extra departments to the core business. This set the pattern for what we now know as "major multiples", the big names you find in most shopping centres nowadays. Brixton was where David Greig opened his first shop, at 54 Atlantic Road, c. 1870. This expanded into two adjoining shops, while the firm eventually had other Central Brixton shops in Station Road and in Electric Avenue.

A postcard illustrating Morley's store immediately after their fire, August 1910. (Linskey collection)

Electric Avenue itself opened in 1888 as the first shopping street to be lit by electricity, the lamps being suspended under a glazed cast iron canopy over the pavements on both sides of the road. Like some modern centres, it had a slow start, until the developer persuaded David Greig to take premises there and act as a "magnet" to attract more shoppers and shopkeepers. It is evident from old postcards that by the turn of the century, Electric Avenue was really the focal point of Brixton as a shopping centre, with its Christmas decorations far more spectacular than we have seen in recent times.

4.4 More than just Shopping

Brixton's burgeoning Centre rapidly acquired many of the other amenities of a small town. By 1888, it boasted two public halls, the Angell Town Institution in Gresham Road (now the Abeng Centre) and the Brixton Hall in Acre Lane (opposite the present Town Hall).

Both Liberal and Conservative parties had their own club premises in the area. In 1893 a public library was opened, paid for by Sir Henry Tate. The Brixton Theatre was built on an adjoining site the next year, and a second, the Empress, opened in 1898 in Brighton Terrace, off Brixton Road. The Brixton Theatre generally offered plays while the Empress usually presented variety shows, though both would have their Christmas pantomime season.

Roller skating was one of the crazes in the early years of this century, and

Morley's staff assemble behind the store in Bernays Grove prior to a coach outing, late 1930s. (Linskey collection)

Brixton Liberal Club, 1-3 Effra Road, in 1885. Adapted from a pair of houses built c.1810, the premises were later used as a public hall (Raleigh Hall), then as a private school, and more recently as workshops. (Lambeth Archives)

around 1910 a rink opened at the corner of Brixton Water Lane and Tulse Hill. (It closed about 1965, eventually re-opening as a carpet store, which was rebuilt in 1986.) Between 1910 and 1938 a greyhound racing track operated in Brixton Road, on the present site of St.Helen's School (opposite Max Roach Park). During the late 1930s, a site at the corner of Effra and Saltoun Roads was shared by a Fun Fair and a coach station, the base of Orange Luxury Coaches.

Between 1910 and 1915, at least 9 cinemas opened in the Brixton area, though some - in railway arches for example - proved short-lived as safety legislation was tightened up. The sole survivor of this first generation still in cinema use is the Ritzy in Brixton Oval, recently restored and extended. Others included the present London Electricity office in Brixton Road, and the Rex in Brixton Hill, of which just the front portion survives as a camping shop.

In the late 1920s, the introduction of sound resulted in a second generation of larger and more impressive cinemas, challenging the earlier "flea-pits". In Brixton this phase is represented by the Astoria (now the Academy) opened in 1929, with an interior design reminiscent of an Italian garden, complete with starlit night sky overhead. Live shows were offered as well as films, and perhaps this new competition led to the Empress Theatre undergoing an "art deco" style facelift in 1931.

4.5 Interwar Investment

The local population continued to increase in the late 19th century as better horsebus and tram services improved access to the Brixton area, and more streets of small houses filled up the backlands.

From the turn of the century, the first generation of suburban villas began to disappear as their leases fell in, to be replaced by smaller houses or flats at a greater density. This process accelerated after the First World War, with the "carriage trade" leaving the area and in any case having to cope with far fewer domestic servants.

As a shopping centre though, Brixton still enjoyed good access from a wide catchment area, as well as a growing local population, so the loss of the higher earners was not yet a problem. In 1925, Brixton could claim to be South London's largest and best shopping centre, and in fact, the interwar period saw increased investment in improving the shopping facilities.

In 1926-27 Quin & Axtens rebuilt their store between Ferndale and Stockwell Roads in a classical style. In 1928 British Home Stores chose

The Empress Theatre after its 1931 remodelling. (Lambeth Archives)

Playbill for the Empress Theatre, October 14, 1910. (Herne Hill Society)

Brixton for their first store (albeit in an adapted Victorian building, now Superdrug). Marks & Spenser too built their present store in the 1930s, replacing earlier premises used by the Exchange Stores of Francis & Son.

South of the railway bridges, the London County Council were finding it increasingly difficult to restrain commercial development on the long front gardens of Brixton Place, on the east side of Brixton Road. In 1935, agreement was reached between the LCC and the frontagers that the 1810 building line could be moved forward, provided that the front half of the original gardens was surrendered to the LCC to allow widening of the road. As a result, most of the frontage between the high level viaduct and Coldharbour Lane was soon rebuilt, including a new Woolworth's in "Art Deco" style, and a "streamlined" new building for the "Prince of Wales" public house.

Further south, the Town Hall, St.Matthew's Church and Oval Gardens blocked any southward expansion of the shopping centre, which instead folded back on itself with many small shops concentrated in a compact area.

4.6 Street Market & Arcades

A street market developed outside the railway station in Atlantic Road during the 1870s. By 1881, the street was lined with both shops and market stalls, and Lambeth Council made an ineffective attempt to ban the stalls because of the crowds. An account written just before the opening of Electric Avenue describes the Atlantic Road market thus:

"A little more than a dozen years ago, it was a quiet, rather out-of-the-way thoroughfare of private houses. These are now all altered into shops, which seem to have crystallised themselves into every conceivable corner of this favoured situation. On Saturday evenings crowds of people, mostly of the working class element, may be seen wandering about the roadway between the costermongers' barrows and the stalls of the various vendors, laying out their money in the purchase of provisions for the week. Not only are articles of prime necessity sold here, but those of taste and luxury are also to be found displayed to tempt the passer-by. Grapes and tomatoes may be bought for threepence a pound and sometimes even for twopence. In the spring and summer months, flowers and plants are extensively sold and in great variety.

And in almost as great variety may be seen that indigenous product of crowds, the beggar. But as begging is not permitted, most of them shelter themselves behind a performance of some kind, musical or otherwise. Here may be seen every week the two women who sing Moody and Sankey's hymns to a concertina accompaniment - the one-armed man who grinds away at a barrel organ - the respectably clad old gentleman who silently offers matches for sale - besides every kind of street musician and many others - amongst which may be seen the blind man whose card informs the public that he has been 'blind for several years with a family of seven children, the result of an accident.'"

Cover illustration from the souvenir programme for the opening of the Astoria Cinema, 19 August 1929. It continues in use for live performances as The Academy. (Lambeth Archives)

In 1921, to allow traffic to flow freely, the police finally moved stallholders to Brixton Station Road and Pope's Road. To cope with demand, market stalls were eventually allowed into Electric Avenue in 1949, despite the shopkeepers' objections to the associated rubbish.

The covered arcades are relatively recent: Reliance Arcade was built in 1929, on the site of one house in Brixton Road (the shell is still there above the arcade) linking to its former Mews in Electric Lane.

Market Row followed 2 years later (1931) and the Granville Arcade was developed by a Mr Granville Grossman in 1937. These arcades provided a step up for market traders, in the form of small lock-up shops without accommodation above, but it also meant that many traders might no longer live locally.

CHAPTER 5 - SOCIAL CHANGE

5.1 A Metropolitan Role

Since Elizabethan times, each parish church had been responsible for the relief of poor residents of the parish, levying a rate or tax on all land and buildings within the parish. This system, supplemented by various charitable bequests, was administered by the churchwardens or Parish Vestry (from the room in the church where they originally met). Despite the opening of additional churches in the Brixton area, the Parish Council or Vestry continued to be based on the original parish of St.Mary's Church, adjoining Lambeth Palace.

In 1855 Parliament made the vestries into independent administrative bodies, free of any church or denominational ties, and created the Metropolitan Board of Works to oversee major public works for the built-up area as a whole, already comprising 3 million people. Further changes were soon needed to cope with the problems of this rapidly-growing city, or as the Victorians termed it, Metropolis. In 1889 the London County Council (LCC) was created, replacing the Metropolitan Board of Works with a more powerful body covering a wider area. Then in 1904, the LCC also took over the functions of the London School Board.

As Lambeth's population increased, the Vestry had grown in number to 120 vestrymen. These were replaced by 60 councillors in 1899 when another London Government Act created Metropolitan Boroughs in place of the old vestries. The new Council soon wanted a more substantial replacement for its 1852 Vestry Hall near Kennington Cross. Despite vocal opposition from the north of the borough, it opted to move to Brixton, by then a dynamic commercial centre and at the midpoint of the new borough. A site was acquired in 1904 and the new Town Hall was opened by the Prince of Wales (later King George V) on 29 April 1908. It was extended in 1937-38, to include an assembly hall in Acre Lane and a new top floor in place of the original slate roof.

5.2 Promoting Local Health

Gradually public authorities took on more of the services which had originally been provided only by churches and charities. In matters of health, it was local authorities which took the lead until the National Health Service was created in 1948, and facilities like health clinics remained under local control until 1974.

The Brixton Dispensary was founded in 1850 in private rooms by a Dr.Wray, "to afford medical and surgical aid to necessitous persons in Brixton, Herne Hill and Tulse Hill." It was financed from donations and subscriptions: each subscriber received 12 letters of recommendation, which he or she could distribute to deserving cases, to enable them to receive medical attention at minimum cost. Further income came from "patients' pence" - one penny was charged per prescription.

About 1890, new premises were built at 19 Brixton Water Lane, with a small extension added in 1916. Between the two World Wars, it was increasingly supported by the LCC, but with the creation of the National Health Service, the Dispensary closed and the building was taken over for use as a child guidance clinic.

The South-Western Hospital was built in Landor Road in 1869-70 to receive patients suffering from fever and smallpox. Medical skills were still limited, and the main aim was to limit the spread of epidemics among poorer communities by isolating infectious cases. The hospital was one of a number established for this purpose by the Metropolitan Asylums Board, whose duties were eventually taken over by the LCC in 1930.

The Brixton Dispensary provided cheap medical care for the needy before the advent of the National Health Service. These premises were opened in Brixton Water Lane in 1890. (Linskey Collection)

5.3 Extending Education

Education depended very much on the churches and private schools until the London School Board got into its stride in the last quarter of the 19th century. The Board was set up to meet the requirement for compulsory schooling introduced by Parliament in 1870. This was achieved by the construction of new schools based on standard designs, usually substantial 3-storey buildings - boys on the top floor, girls on the first floor, and "mixed infants" on the ground floor. Several examples survive around Brixton, such as Santley Street, off Ferndale Road, though most have experienced changes of name and age range over the past century.

As more Board Schools opened, providing free education, some of the fee-paying private and church schools closed due to the competition. However, the Stockwell Grammar School closed in more unusual circumstances, for in 1872 the headmaster was convicted of murder!

On 8th October 1871, 67 year-old John Selby Watson killed his wife Ann at their home, 28 St.Martin's Road, Stockwell. Watson was tried and convicted at the Old Bailey the following January. The trial attracted much publicity, partly because of Watson's position as a professional man, and as a scholar and author. His numerous works included translations of Roman writers such as Lucretius, and original works such as "Geology; a Poem in

Stockwell College, which trained schoolmistresses for the British and Foreign Schools Society, was demolished for the building of the Stockwell Gardens Estate in the 1930s. (Linskey Collection)

Seven Books" of 1844. The trial, in which many people, including the Vicar of nearby St.Andrew's Church, gave evidence, was notable because Watson escaped the death penalty on the grounds of insanity - one of the first convicted murderers to do so. He spent the rest of his life in gaol, dying in Parkhurst Prison in 1884.

Dr Watson was not the proprietor, only an employee of the trustees, but the scandal was too much for a school in what was then felt to be a genteel neighbourhood. With competition from Board schools, and more of Stockwell being developed as working class housing, the Grammar School closed and was eventually replaced by new houses, now numbers 15b-19c Stockwell Park Road.

The Brixton area saw a number of innovations in vocational education. Stockwell College was opened in Stockwell Road in 1861, by the British and Foreign Schools Society. Its purpose was to train schoolmistresses for the "British Schools" sponsored by nonconformist churches. The addition of a cookery school in 1897 brought the number of trainees up to 800, of whom 150 were residential. It included a "practising school" with its own pupils for the students to gain practical experience. In 1935 it moved to Bromley, and the site was later developed as part of the Stockwell Gardens Estate.

Its Anglican counterpart was St.Gabriel's College in Cormont Road, facing Myatt's Fields Park and built in 1899-1903. It was founded by Canon Charles Edward Brooke as a Church of England college for women teachers. By the 1980s it had been amalgamated with Goldsmith's College, and operated as their Millard annexe until c.1987. The building was then briefly used for a commercial accountancy college, but after a long period of disuse, conversion to flats was approved.

5.4 The School of Building

In 1874, the Surrey County Club had been erected as a private venture on open land at the west end of Shepherd's Lane (now 140 Ferndale Road). The buildings included a swimming pool, but the venture failed in 1881, and the premises were next used for Lambeth Polytechnic School, organised by a local committee. By 1892, this too had closed and the site was acquired by Lambeth Vestry, for new baths and washhouses, but the proposed scheme was too expensive, so the premises were still on the market in 1897, when the London County Council took up the idea of a technical school for the building industry.

Despite a strong local campaign in support of the new proposal, purchase negotiations were not completed until 1901. The former swimming pool hall was then adapted, so that classes could commence in January 1904, with the official opening of the LCC Brixton School of Building in February.

A school of architecture was added in 1906, directed until 1928 by Beresford Pite (designer of Christ Church, North Brixton). A four-storey block was built alongside the railway in 1908-9, and at the same time a "Junior Day Technical School" was opened for 50 boys aged 13 upwards and preparing to enter the building industry. By 1938 this had increased to 315 boys, but in 1956 it was incorporated in the new Tulse Hill Comprehensive School.

Early emphasis was on evening classes, but a Senior Day School was started in 1912, and expanded in scope and numbers between the two World Wars, to provide 3-year courses in the main building professions. A former colleague who studied at the school in the 1930s recalled that the architecture course included practical instruction in all the building trades, as well as academic and technical subjects.

The School of Building was originally entered through a house in Ferndale Road, converted as offices, but in 1935 this was replaced by another classroom block fronting the road. In 1947 the former Brixton Orphanage in Barrington Road was taken over to provide more space for the Building Trades Department. In the 1960s the former Sussex Road School (now Hillmead Junior) was also taken over to accommodate some of the professional courses. In 1970 the School was merged with other institutions to form the Polytechnic of the South Bank, but the building trade courses were hived off to Vauxhall Technical College. All courses then moved to long-awaited new buildings in Wandsworth Road from September 1974, though the Ferndale Road site continues in use, by Lambeth College.

5.5 Electrifying Transport

The original "Underground" railways of London had been of "cut and cover" construction, using adapted steam trains to link the main railway termini while minimising the cost of compensation for the property they traversed. The first true "Tube" line, and the first to use electric power, was the City and South London Line, linking King William Street to Stockwell through deep tunnels. The line was opened in 1890, and carried 165,000 passengers in its first 2 weeks. It rapidly gained popularity for being quick, clean and cheap, with a flat fare of 2d.

Sidings were originally sited on what is now the Stockwell Gardens Estate. Steep ramps were provided to raise the rolling stock 12 metres to the surface level for maintenance. Early proposals for branches to Brixton and Loughborough Junction were not followed up, but the line was extended south-west, first to Clapham Common (1900) and on to Morden in 1926. It was linked with the Hampstead and Highgate Railway in 1924, becoming the Northern Line in 1937.

The first surface-level railway line to be electrified was the South London Line between Victoria and London Bridge, in 1909. This used 6600 volt overhead cables, and local access was at East Brixton Station, the line passing over the main Brixton Station at high level on its way to Victoria.

The first electric trams in London were introduced on the route from Westminster Bridge to Tooting, running along the Clapham Road through Stockwell. The service was inaugurated on 15 May 1903 by the Prince of Wales (later King George V). The electric current was supplied through a narrow conduit laid in the road between the 2 rails. The same method was the logical choice in the following year to replace the cable drive on the Brixton Road route. However overhead wires were installed on some

One of the cable trams which ran along Brixton Road before the route was electrified in 1904. (Pamlin Prints)

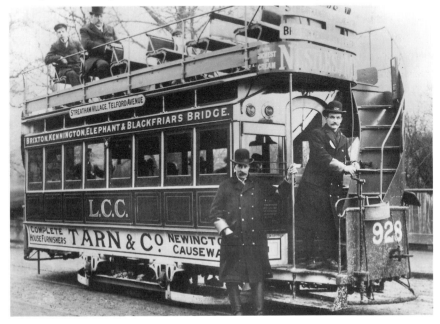

existing tram routes, including via Gresham Road and Coldharbour Lane to Loughborough Junction. They were also used for the last line to be completed in the area, linking Brixton to Herne Hill via Effra and Dulwich Roads in 1912.

5.6 Eminent Edwardians

Brixton's more famous residents of the late 19th and early 20th century fall into two distinct groups, reflecting the social divisions of the area. In the grand houses fronting roads such as Tulse Hill and Brixton Hill, we find those who were already successful, while among the humbler terraces, apartment blocks and boarding houses, we find those taking their first steps towards fame. Only in a few cases have the original buildings survived to carry a plaque, and almost all of the grander houses have been swept away.

Sir William Huggins built a house at 90 Upper Tulse Hill in 1855-56. Son of a successful silk mercer in the City, he was able to devote much of his time to his interest in astronomy. From his own observatory attached to the house, he was the first to use spectrographic analysis to determine the composition of stars and comets, and established that nebulae were clouds of gas. He was knighted in 1897, and died in 1910.

His neighbours were more likely to be involved in commerce than science or the arts. Even after the First World War, residents of Tulse Hill still included Mr Pears of Pears Soap, Mr Lovell of Lovell & Christmas, and Mr Knight of the surveyors Knight, Frank & Rutley.

Local artistic connections are fleeting. The water colour artist David Cox (1783-1859) lived at 34 Foxley Road, Holland Town, from 1827-41. His son, David Cox junior (b.1809), was active as a local artist and lived for a time at 2 New Park Road, at the top of Brixton Hill. The Pre-Raphaelite artist Ford Maddox Brown had his studio at Stockwell in the 1850s. The lithographers Louis Haghe (1806-1885) and his brother Carl (or Charles) lived at 103 Stockwell Road.

A blue plaque on 87 Hackford Road marks where Vincent Van Gogh stayed in 1873-74 while working at his uncle's print gallery in Southampton Street, off the Strand. The 20-year old Vincent fell in love with his landlady's daughter, Eugenie, but she was already engaged to a previous lodger and, rebuffed, he had to find other lodgings at Kennington. Van Gogh did not take up painting fully until 1882, but a simple sketch he made of Hackford Road was found among Eugenie's effects after her death.

The writer Henry Havelock Ellis (1859-1939) is commemorated by a plaque on Dover Mansions in Canterbury Crescent. He grew up in the Surrey outskirts of London but spent four years as a teacher in Australia before returning to study medicine at St.Thomas's Hospital in 1881. He first took up writing to support himself during his studies, and his main output consisted of popular books on science and the arts. He is chiefly remembered though for pioneering the scientific study of sex with his "Studies in the Psychology of Sex" published in seven volumes from 1897-1928. He lived at Dover Mansions from 1909 until 1927, when he retired to Sussex.

Home Secretary Herbert Morrison MP (centre) visiting Lambeth Town Hall to discuss Civil Defence arrangements, 24 August 1944. On the left is the Mayor, Alderman W.Lockyer, who remained in office throughout the war. (Lambeth Archives)

Herbert Morrison (1888-1965) was born at 240 Ferndale Road, next to what was then the Brixton Fire Station. In 1895 the family moved a short distance to 39 Mordaunt Street. Herbert went to the Board School in Stockwell Road, and later to St.Andrew's School in Lingham Street. He first became involved in politics by joining the Brixton branch of the Independent Labour Party in 1906, but work and politics took him across London, to become Mayor of Hackney in 1919 and its MP in 1923. He went on to become Minister of Transport in 1929, leader of Labour's first majority on the London County Council in 1934, Home Secretary in the Wartime Coalition Cabinet, and a leading member of the 1945-51 Labour Cabinet. He never forgot his roots, and on taking a life peerage in 1959 he became Lord Morrison of Lambeth.

5.7 The First World War

The First World War brought little direct destruction to the area, but did set in motion some profound social changes which were to have a major impact later. There were several bombing raids over London by Zeppelins, some of which affected Brixton. Despite the shock effect, the actual damage was slight by the standards of the Second World War. Most of the sites affected were close to Brixton Hill, which the pilots could pick out readily among the maze of streets below them.

Civilian building work almost came to a halt, and numbers at the Brixton School of Building fell sharply. From 1915 the School was also training munition workers of various kinds, while propeller blades and wing ribs for aeroplanes were being made in its woodwork shops. St.Gabriel's College was pressed into use as a military hospital (the 1st London General Hospital) with additional accommodation provided in temporary huts across the road in Myatt's Fields Park.

Motor buses had appeared just before the War, and wartime production of motor transport greatly speeded up its acceptance. Among other local contributions to the war effort, the Bon Marche store donated three of its "motor pantechnicons" as army transport. The railways were already feeling the competition from buses and trams for shorter journeys. As a result, the railway companies took a critical look at their suburban services. In 1916 the London & South-Western Railway, using the War as an excuse, closed their Elephant & Castle to Brixton services, including one remarkable service from Ludgate Hill via Brixton and Chelsea to Richmond and Twickenham. Camberwell and Walworth Road stations were closed, as were the intermediate stops on the Victoria to Brixton line, and the platforms at Loughborough Junction serving the spur to Brixton and Peckham.

5.8 Housing Changes

Most housing built in the Brixton area up to 1914 had been in the form of family houses for renting. It was common practice for anyone who came into some money, from a successful business transaction or a legacy, to purchase several such houses so that the rents would continue to provide an income for the future.

However, the onset of the First World War brought an end to house-building, and rents were soon frozen by government order. One lasting effect of these rent controls was to start a long slow decline in the standard of privately-rented housing, as landlords skimped repairs to compensate for lower incomes from controlled rents, or squeezed more tenants into a house to increase short-term profits, resulting in greater wear and tear on the common parts.

Zeppelin Raid damage in Baytree Road, off Brixton Hill, in September 1916. (Lambeth Archives)

Even before the end of the 19th century, the larger houses around Brixton were tending to be used as boarding houses or let as separate floors or rooms, particularly areas like Angell Town and Loughborough Park. With good access to Central London by public transport, performers in the West End Music Halls appreciated being able to get back to home or lodgings after the show, using the late-night trams. There was also strong demand from young shop-workers employed locally.

Between the two World Wars, the people for whom these larger houses had been intended, the large Victorian merchant families with resident servants, became a rarity. London's economy between the Wars was more buoyant than the rest of the country, offering more attractive employment than domestic service. Those who could still afford a retinue of servants, could also afford to move to more rural surroundings, whence they could travel to the City by train, or increasingly by car.

All this coincided with the expiry of the original 99-year leases on many of the early-19th century houses. These houses and their often generous grounds provided a tempting opportunity for builders who could replace them with streets of smaller houses for owner-occupiers (such as Baytree Road) or the newly-fashionable blocks of privately-rented service flats. These (such as Tudor Close in Brixton Hill, with its own swimming pool and tennis courts) were aimed at a younger generation, single people and couples, rather than the extended Victorian household and its servants.

Acre Lane Motor Engineers & driving school, 1933. Between the two World Wars, many motor businesses set up along the main roads leading out of Brixton. (Linskey Collection)

Local authority involvement in housing had become possible after the Housing of the Working Classes Act in 1901. The first example in Brixton was the construction of Briscoe's buildings (now Renton Close) by the LCC in Brixton Hill. After the First World War, the increased finance available under the 1919 Housing Act enabled the LCC to join in the redevelopment process, going on to build blocks of flats in Loughborough Road, Cowley Road and Tulse Hill during the 1930s. With the motivation of both the LCC and private developers being to accommodate more people on their sites, it is no surprise that the population of Lambeth as a whole reached its peak in the 1930s.

5.9 Commerce & Industry

Brixton lacked large-scale industry, having begun as a residential suburb. The arrival of the railways, and then of horse-bus and tram services, had made it a more popular "dormitory" from which even more people could commute to work in Central London. Most local employment was in the shopping centre, and to a lesser extent in smaller enterprises and workshops, often interspersed among the houses.

In this period, sites along the major roads proved popular for new commercial uses, even the occasional "art deco" style factory building like the Sunlight Laundry in Acre Lane. In its heyday the Sunlight Laundry employed over 700 people and provided exemplary staff facilities, in contrast to the old Victorian "sweatshops".

A large printing works was established in Clapham Road before the First World War (used in recent years for Freemans mail order goods) and Sharwoods Pickles operated a factory nearby in Offley Road until the mid-1960s. In the 1920s the Brixton Estate Company built a factory development at the northern end of Brixton Road, the first of many industrial estates which the firm has continued to build and manage around the country. The Royal Arsenal Co-operative Society had a large bakery in Brixton Hill (demolished in 1973 to make way for Council offices, now Olive Morris House). Several large garages were established in the Brixton area before the Second World War, and Allard cars were briefly built in Acre Lane.

5.10 Another War

The Second World War set the pattern for a more interventionist style of local government. Education, social services, the fire brigade and some health services continued to be provided by the LCC, but Lambeth Borough Council suddenly found itself administering many new war-time responsibilities such as civil defence and emergency rehousing.

At the outbreak of war, over 225,000 gas masks were distributed, and air raid shelters provided for 130,000 people. Due to the difficulty of protecting the mass of the population from air raids, massive evacuations were organised, particularly of children. A new Information Centre was opened in Acre Lane, opposite the Town Hall, to handle the vastly increased number of enquiries from members of the public.

Contemporary press reports of air raid damage were limited by wartime censorship, and so are of little help to the historian. Figures are only readily available for Lambeth as a whole, which then included Vauxhall and Norwood in addition to Brixton. The first bomb was dropped in Lambeth on 29 August 1940, and from then until July 1941 there were 579 air raid alerts, resulting in 2,131 incidents of air raid damage. The most severe raid was on the night of 16/17 April 1941, resulting in 234 people killed and 278 injured. Notable casualties of the 1940/41 "Blitz" were the Brixton Theatre (destroyed 8th November 1940) and Quin & Axtens department store (destroyed May 1941). Further north in Brixton Road, a bomb crater

Brixton Prison after a near miss by a German V1 flying bomb, 19 June 1944. (Lambeth Archives)

exposed the River Effra to public view again.

From August to December 1941, no bombs were dropped in the borough, the bulk of the German Air Force then being engaged in Russia. A more limited German campaign between April and October 1942 produced 25 alerts, but no damage. Again in 1943 the air raid sirens were sounded on 98 occasions, but no bombs fell in Lambeth and damage was confined to that from falling anti-aircraft shells.

The German Air Force became more active again between January and May 1944, with 102 bombs being recorded as falling in the borough, plus the smaller incendiary bombs.

The V1 and V2 "revenge weapons", each carrying a tonne of explosive, launched a new wave of airborne destruction, from June 1944 to January 1945. Misinformation fed back to the German forces meant that most fell short of their aiming point in Central London, but South London and its fringes suffered more as a result. In Lambeth as a whole, 95 V1 flying bombs resulted in 250 people dead and 709 seriously injured. 74 V1s actually fell within the borough boundary.

By far the worst single incident in Brixton was on 28 June 1944, when the

Brixton's worst single air raid incident occurred on 28 June 1944, when a flying bomb fell on the Council's Information Centre in Acre Lane, causing many casualties and also badly damaging the adjoining Christian Science Church, seen beyond. (Lambeth Archives)

busy Information Centre opposite the Town Hall was hit, also destroying the nearby Post Office and badly damaging the adjoining church.

Only 2 of the V2 rockets fell within Lambeth, but another 3 falling nearby contributed to the damage and casualties - 41 killed and 62 injured in all.

With most of the children evacuated during the war, many schools were used for Civil Defence purposes. Sudbourne Road, Effra Parade, Hackford Road, Cormont Road and Lingham Street (St.Andrew's) Schools were all used as temporary fire stations by the Auxiliary Fire Service. Sussex Road (now Hillmead) School was being used as a rest centre for bombed-out families when visited by King George VI and Queen Elizabeth on 29 June 1944.

To provide direct protection, official policy preferred many small and modest air raid shelters, rather than large well-protected structures. Perhaps the fear was that people would be reluctant to emerge after a raid to continue their work, so public shelters were generally basic brick and concrete structures at ground level.

Families with gardens could have an Anderson shelter, a miniature hut of corrugated iron, earthed over. For those without, the Morrison shelter was introduced, a wire-mesh safety cage which would provide some protection if the house collapsed around the occupants.

Eventually, fears that Germany might develop an atomic bomb prompted work on a series of deep shelters along the Northern Line in 1940-42, consisting of paired tunnels above the platforms of selected Tube stations. In practice, most of these were only used for military purposes. The shelter at Stockwell Station is marked by a concrete drum (for the lift shaft, stairs and ventilation grilles) poignantly sited next to the clock tower memorial to Lambeth's dead in the First World War.

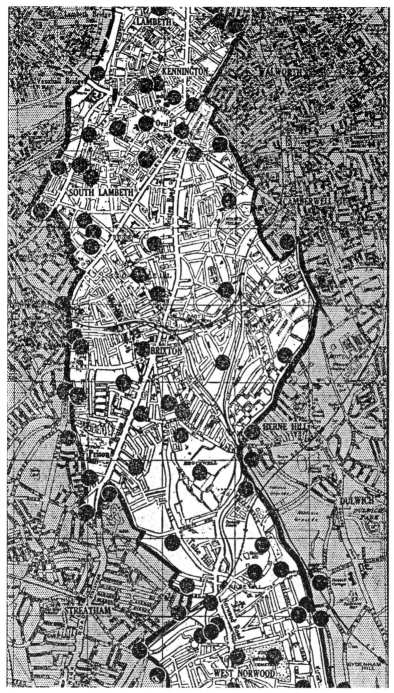

Part of a map published by the "Evening News" after the flying bomb campaign, showing where these early guided missiles fell in Central Lambeth. (Lambeth Archives)

CHAPTER 6 - INTO DECLINE

6.1 The Housing Crisis

Immediately after the Second World War, there was a severe housing shortage in London as a result of war damage, combined with families returning after war service or evacuation. For the first time there was even some squatting of abandoned houses. Compared with some other parts of London, bomb damage in Brixton from the 1939-45 war was piecemeal, but it set in motion programmes to rebuild the damaged areas as Council housing, mostly as blocks of flats.

Privately-rented housing had been in a long slow decline since the introduction of rent controls during the First World War. Houses were no longer being built for rent, so the stock was shrinking and ageing. This decline became more marked in the 1950s, with the supply of privately-rented housing being reduced by sales to owner-occupiers on the one hand, and by local authority slum clearance on the other.

In some streets, conditions worsened as the original building leases neared their end, with the leaseholders attempting to wring a few more pounds from their tenants while the opportunity remained, before the property reverted to the ground landlord.

Yet Brixton continued to provide a foothold for those coming to London in search of work, and during the fifties and sixties landlords found a ready market among immigrants from the Commonwealth, notably Jamaica. At a time when imperial, even racist, attitudes predominated, rooms were a little easier to obtain around Brixton, which already had a tradition of providing theatrical "digs". In addition, the Mayor, supported by the local MP, Marcus Lipton, hosted a few events to welcome the first arrivals from the West Indies. Later arrivals preferred to come to districts like this where they might find relatives or former neighbours already established.

6.2 Searching for Solutions

Against this background, Council housing programmes were expanded.

The LCC and its successor, the Greater London Council, were also able to offer people housing outside the borough, or even outside London itself. In the meantime, the more prosperous of Brixton's residents preferred to buy their own homes in newer suburbs on London's fringes, so in all, many people were leaving Brixton behind.

Expanded as a London Borough in 1965, Lambeth Council moved on to larger-scale house-building projects, trying various building forms to maximise the number of tenants on each site. At first system-built tower blocks were thought to be the answer, though with hindsight we can be thankful that the 50-storey tower blocks designed for the centre of Brixton stayed on the drawing board. The next approach used more complex "medium-rise" layouts like the Stockwell Park and Angell Town estates, which proved difficult to manage in their original form. By the mid-70s the Council began to realise that terraced houses were just as effective in using the land, while being cheaper to build and more attractive to tenants.

By this time, the Council's policy of rebuilding whole neighbourhoods was meeting increasing opposition from local people resenting the loss of their homes and the break-up of communities. With Central Government concerned at the rising cost of the redevelopment programme, several areas around Brixton were reprieved from the bulldozer. The emphasis was belatedly placed on the improvement of the existing housing, but after years of blight and neglect, the backlog of repairs was immense.

The number of empty houses awaiting demolition during the height of the redevelopment programme in the early 70s led to the recurrence of

Commercial uses gradually took over what were once elegant villas along Brixton Road, with the front gardens turned into car parks. Photographed c.1965, the buildings and the businesses were swept away ten years later to create Max Roach Park.
(Lambeth Archives)

One of the last trams, here with overhead wires, seen in May 1951 at the junction of Dalberg Road and Brixton Water Lane. The site to the right is derelict after war damage. (Pamlin Prints)

Barrington Road, photographed c.1960, showing the New Loughborough Estate, built by the London County Council. (Lambeth Archives)

squatting. Some squatter groups eventually became housing co-ops or associations, to play an active part in the rehabilitation of old housing, such as Villa Road.

Since the mid-60s, Lambeth Council had been identifying existing buildings for conservation or rehabilitation, but at first this was limited to small pockets of early 19th century buildings for their architectural merit alone. Gradually the merits of retaining larger areas, and of re-using a wider range of old buildings, gained acceptance, albeit against a background of diminishing public funds.

6.3 Decline of the Shopping Centre

The shopping centre as such did not suffer major damage in the Second World War, the biggest casualty being Quin & Axtens on Brixton Road. The shell of their premises was refurbished c.1950 as government offices with a series of individual shops below, and is much the same today.

At first there was complacency, as other centres had suffered more severely, but Brixton had been built in the era of the horsevan and handcart, and was ill-prepared for growing car ownership and deliveries from ever-larger lorries. The main roads which had previously been a magnet to

Town Centre, as proposed in 1969 – view from south with tower blocks, from Lambeth Council report. (Brixton Society collection)

shoppers increasingly became barriers as traffic increased, particularly along the A23 Brixton Road, which divided the quality stores on the west side from the market area on the east.

As other areas rebuilt in the postwar period, they could provide for these problems, and those further out could benefit from a growing and relatively prosperous population, as Brixton had done 80 years earlier. Meanwhile, Brixton's own population was declining both in numbers and in purchasing power. The better-off preferred to move further out of London, with an inevitable effect on the number and quality of shops which the remaining population could support.

Lambeth Council attempted to respond to changing conditions with ambitious plans for rebuilding the Centre on modern lines. The first proposals were drawn up in 1963, based on bold concepts which were only abandoned as impractical 20 years later - wholesale rebuilding to the Council's plan, with ground-level traffic separated from pedestrian movement at a higher level.

Successive versions of the master plan emerged in 1967, 1969, 1975 and 1980, scaling down the extent of rebuilding each time, but the plans were not revised quickly enough to adapt to changing market conditions, and

1974 proposals for a new shopping centre and housing between Coldharbour Lane and Kellett Road, viewed from above St. Matthew's churchyard.
(Architects' Journal, 20.3.74)

consistently failed to attract private investment. Only the largest investors or developers would be able to fund this comprehensive development approach, but they could find more profitable sites elsewhere, where retail trade was still growing.

Little thought was given to the role of existing shopkeepers or new businesses, so that smaller-scale investment was effectively discouraged. Even routine maintenance was forgone, in the expectation that most of the buildings would be coming down in the near future. The effect was to aggravate the decline through "Planning Blight", depriving the area of commercial investment for some 20 years.

The opening of the long-awaited Tube link in 1971 seemed only to make it easier for local people to get to the West End, rather than bring in more shoppers. In addition, east-west links were diminished with the closure of East Brixton station in 1976. At least Brixton escaped the intrusion of the motorway network planned by the GLC. At the beginning of the 1970s, the planning of Brixton's Town Centre was dominated by an elevated motorway or "Ringway" set to cross Brixton from east to west. Its one tangible result was the 9-storey "barrier block" of Southwyck House in Coldharbour Lane, intended to screen the Moorland Road Estate from the noise of the motorway, though the road was cancelled in the same month as the block was started!

A 1985 survey by chartered surveyors Hillier Parker illustrates Brixton's decline against other London centres, ranking them by the number of "multiple" retailers with branches there. On this basis, Brixton ranked 3rd among London Shopping Centres in 1961, and slipped to 9th in 1971. The 1976 Greater London Development Plan classified it as one of 27 strategic centres, but by 1984 Hillier Parker ranked it as not 27th but 37th! (having assessed 56 London shopping centres in all).

6.4 Political Life

With such major issues to be tackled in post-war Brixton, it is worth a glance at the local political scene. Brixton had been the seat of Lambeth's local government since the Town Hall was opened in 1908, but as early as 1885 it had become a constituency with its own Member of Parliament. In early years, it generally returned a Conservative MP, apart from two brief periods of Liberal success in 1906-10 and 1923-24. In 1945, in line with the national swing, the seat was won for Labour by Marcus Lipton, who had already gained local recognition as the first Jewish Alderman on Lambeth

Council in 1937. He retained the seat until boundary changes merged it with Clapham in 1974, and continued as MP for the new "Lambeth Central" seat until his death in 1978.

Throughout this time, the South-Eastern quarter of Brixton remained part of the Norwood parliamentary constituency, enlarged to include Angell Town when Lambeth's declining population resulted in "Lambeth Central" being absorbed into adjoining constituencies. This change also brought the South-Western quarter (Town Hall ward) into the Streatham constituency, leaving the rest of Brixton as part of an enlarged Vauxhall constituency.

Under the pressures of wartime emergencies and post-war reconstruction, the Labour-led Lambeth Council had developed a paternalistic approach to its residents. In 1965 it took on extra functions from the former LCC, while Clapham and Streatham were added to its territory, including the southern part of Brixton Hill from Upper Tulse Hill onwards. A new Greater London Council floated above the boroughs in a loosely-defined strategic role, which could work well when the Borough Council and GLC were of like minds, but which led to friction whenever they were controlled by different political parties.

At the 1968 Council elections, the Conservatives gained control, helped by established support in the recently-added districts of Streatham and Clapham. There may have been a slowing down of programmes but there was still consensus on many policies. The growing administrative machinery was increasingly in the hands of powerful chief officers, with more services being subsidised - and hence controlled - by Central Government.

In 1971 Labour regained control, with several younger and more radical members joining the Council, particularly from Brixton and Norwood. Traditionally, the role of Councillor or Alderman had fallen to the retired, or to the businessman sufficiently successful to spare the time for his local community. From the 1960s onwards it increasingly drew a younger generation seeking practical experience towards a career in national politics. In their terms, Lambeth Town Hall provided a useful apprenticeship, for in 1995 there were no less than seven former Lambeth Councillors serving as MPs, including Prime Minister John Major and opposition member Ken Livingstone.

John Major was born in 1943 of former theatrical parents. When his father's garden ornament business faltered, they sold their house in Worcester Park and returned to their old music hall haunts in Brixton. Between the ages of 12 and 16, he lived with his family on the top floor of 144 Coldharbour Lane, an old 4-storey house on the Camberwell side of

Loughborough Junction. His first contact with the world of politics was at the age of 13, when Marcus Lipton, the local Labour MP, arranged a visit to the Houses of Parliament. However, not long after leaving school at 16 with disappointing exam results, John joined the local branch of the Young Conservatives.

In Autumn 1959, the family moved to the ground floor of 80 Burton Road, within the Minet Estate. After his father's death, the rest of the family moved away but John took lodgings nearby at 14 Templar Street, where he remained until his marriage in 1970. He was elected to Lambeth Council for Ferndale Ward in 1968, when the Conservatives benefited both from the complacency of the Labour administration and from the low standing of the Labour Government of the time. The pendulum swung back at the next Council election in 1971, but by then John Major had gained his first practical experience of political power as Chairman of Lambeth's Housing Committee.

Ken Livingstone was born in Streatham in 1945, and in the early 1950s lived on the Tulse Hill Estate, the family later moving to a house of their own in West Norwood. Despite both his parents being members of the local Conservative Association, Ken first showed an interest in socialism while attending Tulse Hill Comprehensive School, though he did not actually join the Norwood Labour Party until 1968, at the age of 23.

He was one of the new intake of Labour members to Lambeth Council in 1971, continuing as a Councillor until 1981, when he moved home from Trinity Rise to Camden. In 1973 he was elected to the Greater London Council, which gradually became his main political platform. He became widely known as the leader of the last Labour administration before abolition of the GLC, from 1981 to 1986. At that time his policies were widely criticised as naive and left-wing, but they now seem closer to the municipal socialism of another local predecessor, Herbert Morrison.

6.5 Troubled Times

Successive plans for rebuilding the centre of Brixton had concentrated on shopping and office development as the main ingredients, with a single large Recreation Centre as the sole outlet for leisure needs. Plans for this were unveiled in 1973, but construction was beset by problems, disputes and cost increases, such that the Recreation Centre did not open its doors until 1985.

Lambeth Council planners were slow to recognise the demand for a wider range of entertainment and leisure facilities, or even to acknowledge that

Brixton had acquired a substantial black population. Within the centre of Brixton, planning blight discouraged any substantial new enterprises, while the original entertainment facilities withered away. Around the centre, large areas of old housing were marked down for demolition, with many neighbourhood shops closing as the population fell and shopping habits changed.

In these conditions it was easy for an informal network of unlicensed drinking clubs and meeting places to spring up in run-down shops close to the centre of Brixton, particularly in Railton Road. For residents this produced acute problems from late-night noise, extra traffic, litter and obstruction of access to central Brixton by the customers and their parked cars. As the 1980s dawned, the atmosphere became more tense as illicit drug trading became more blatant, and the area gained an exaggerated reputation for street crime.

Meanwhile, relations between the Black community and the Police had been deteriorating. The launch of a Police "stop and search" campaign against street crime in 1981 soon led to a violent confrontation outside the most notorious "shebeens" in Railton Road, on Saturday 11 April. This developed into a riot which then spread back to the shopping centre itself, with extensive looting and several buildings burnt out.

CHAPTER 7 - NEW DIRECTIONS

7.1 Finding a Way Forward

The possibility of something like Brixton's 1981 riots had been foreseen by the Home Office back in 1974 when it commissioned a series of studies into several "Inner Urban Areas". One of these covered the Stockwell side of Brixton, including the newly-completed Stockwell Park Estate and the neglected older housing on the opposite side of Stockwell Road. The studies highlighted the "Inner City" syndrome: the difficulty of finding good local housing prompting the outward migration of the young and skilled, the resulting accumulation of the unskilled and vulnerable, the decline of local employment and shopping, the weakening of community ties, the neglected environment and the spiral into deprivation and crime.

As a result, the Government launched its "Inner Area Programme" in 1977, with Lambeth as one of a limited number of local councils targeted. The scheme was later extended more widely as the Urban Programme, but at an early stage oversight was transferred from the Home Office to the Department of the Environment, and the original focus on crime prevention and social intervention was lost.

From 1976 onwards, Central Government was trying to restrain local councils' expenditure, and this became more acute for Lambeth after the election of a Conservative Government in 1979. Lambeth's Inner Area Programme therefore put a strong emphasis on physical improvements, partly to continue works which could no longer be funded from the Council's main programme, and partly because successive governments were anxious to provide some relief for a building industry facing a slack period. One innovation of the programme was its "partnership" approach, as a joint initiative not only of Lambeth and the Government, but also the Greater London Council and other statutory bodies such as the health authorities.

Despite the difficult conditions, charitable agencies and community groups were increasingly active in trying to fill gaps left by the shortcomings of Council and Government provision. Churches were becoming prominent again, including newer denominations supported by ethnic minorities. The local population was becoming yet more diverse, with Jamaican immigrants moving further afield and Nigerians becoming more significant. Several refugee and migrant support groups established bases in Brixton.

The contribution of this emerging "Voluntary Sector" was gradually recognised by the authorities, at least as a means of targeting services to vulnerable sections of the population, and by 1980 it too was represented in the "partnership" structure formulating the programme.

Having brought all these service providers together, some attempts were made to review and co-ordinate the delivery of existing services in the area, but without a shared vision or political consensus, these soon petered out. The emphasis therefore remained on selecting new projects to fund.

After the 1981 riots, more effort was made to accommodate proposals from the Voluntary Sector, and several projects were set up to pilot new ideas, but a major limitation soon became apparent. The Urban Programme only provided running costs for 3 years, beyond which projects depended on being adopted as part of mainstream public funding programmes. The burden of these "time-expired" projects became increasingly difficult for Lambeth Council to sustain as its government funding was reduced, and the innovative schemes which did not fit in neatly with established department budgets were the first to be cut back.

During the 1980s, the Government explored various new initiatives to regenerate depressed Inner City areas, such as Enterprise Zones, but Brixton lacked the necessary combination of large ex-industrial sites and commercial development interest. Meanwhile Government thinking was shifting more towards Business as both the engine of renewal and a contributor to the massive costs involved. Finally a new scheme emerged in the form of City Challenge. Local authorities were invited to link up with other agencies and bid in competition, enabling the Government to pick those which seemed to offer most benefits for the public money invested.

After considering Vauxhall as an alternative, Lambeth Council put together a package of proposals for Brixton, which was accepted for the second round of City Challenge funding, starting in April 1993. Whereas the Inner Area Programme covered the whole northern half of Lambeth, down to the South Circular Road, the Challenge boundaries were more tightly drawn, consisting of the Town Centre, major post-war housing estates on its north and east boundaries, and corridors extending out along the main roads which might provide opportunities for new development. Key elements of the Challenge approach were a limited 5-year programme, defined targets to be achieved in that time, using public funds to stimulate other investment, and a new emphasis on partnership by placing management of the programme not with the Council but with a separate Company created for the purpose.

Developing from the steering group of different interests which oversaw the original bid, the Board of the Brixton Challenge Company included Councillors from each party group on the Council, together with representatives of both large and small business interests, the health authority, the police, local community groups and Council tenants' associations. Initially the Housing Corporation also provided a director, but withdrew under Government pressure, to be replaced by another business representative, from larger firms having branches in the area.

Perhaps to avoid scandals like the "marble halls" of the European Bank of Reconstruction, only 4% of Brixton Challenge's own funds could be spent on administration, so it was limited to a small staff team, largely seconded from the Public sector and initially lacking in-house skills in commercial development or public relations. Thus, despite some commercial contributions, the Company remained heavily dependent on the Council for support services and technical advice, but it took time to establish good working relationships.

7.2 The Scarman Report & After

The Inquiry into the 1981 disturbances held most of its sessions in public at the Town Hall. Lord Scarman himself earned much respect in the local community through his patient conduct of the Inquiry, his constructive recommendations, and his continuing support for local initiatives. One of his key recommendations was the establishment of an effective Community/Police Consultative Group, and Lambeth's was set up in 1982, the first in the country. There was much concern over the treatment and welfare of black prisoners after arrest, so another development launched by the Group in 1984 was a panel of lay visitors to monitor custody conditions in the borough's three police stations. Members of Brixton Council of Churches played a key role in making these arrangements work, notably Greta Brooks who later went on to establish the Lambeth Mediation Service, to help ease tensions between neighbours.

The Labour majority at the Town Hall was more ambivalent, preferring a more formal system of local accountability for the Metropolitan Police, involving GLC or borough councillors instead of direct control by the Home Secretary.

A botched police raid on a house in Normandy Road in 1985 resulted in the accidental shooting of its black tenant, Mrs Cherry Groce. A protest outside Brixton Police Station by members of the black community got out of control, and another round of looting broke out. Although the raid had been conducted by another squad without the prior knowledge of Brixton Police, Labour Councillors withdrew their co-operation from the Police and the Consultative Group.

However, dialogue was developing between the Police and the local community through the Consultative Group, sector working parties and neighbourhood watch schemes. Despite the limitations of a police force drawn from very different parts of London, residents were after all concerned about their personal safety and possessions. In the immediate Brixton area, street crime showed a gradual decline from its 1981 peak. Labour Councillors eventually agreed to return to participation in the Consultative Group shortly before the May 1994 Council elections. In practice, co-operation between the Council and the local police had been developing over the previous two years in connection with crime prevention measures in the Brixton Challenge programme. In 1995 with no party in overall control, a police inspector was seconded to assist the Council with crime prevention and safety measures.

7.3 Life Returns

The post-war trend had been for Central Brixton to lose its resident population, while former suburbs like Tulse Hill were gradually rebuilt to house more and more people. The traditional distribution of population was becoming reversed, with the Town Centre in danger of shutting down entirely at night.

Fortunately, this was not to be. There were still enclaves of housing left within the Town Centre, such as the apartment blocks of Rushcroft Road and the cottages of Nursery Road, where residents doggedly resisted official demolition proposals. The lack of commercial interest in "comprehensive redevelopment" left an opportunity for housing associations (and even the occasional developer) to insert new homes or to refurbish existing blocks. As a result, the surviving pockets of housing have been enlarged, renewing the life of the Town Centre.

Nature too has been gradually re-asserting itself, helped perhaps by more sympathetic attitudes in recent times. Thirty or forty years ago, any odd space would be paved, any insect would be sprayed, and the wildlife appeared to be limited to sparrows and pigeons. The neglect of the natural environment was brought home by the Great Storm which struck South-East England in October 1987. Hurricane-force winds felled many of

On Brixton's doorstep, Brockwell Park has been a valuable amenity for such a densely-populated area. It has been increasingly used for major public events, such as the Lambeth Country Show – seen here in 1994. (Brixton Challenge)

View along Effra Road, with Tate Library Gardens on the left. Piece by piece, Rush Common is gradually being restored to create a continuous green corridor along Effra Road and up Brixton Hill. (Brixton Challenge)

Brixton's old-established trees, and the meagre number of younger trees remaining highlighted how little had been done to replace those lost in decades of road-widening and redevelopment.

Since then, greater efforts have been made to establish new trees along the roads and in local open spaces, and to encourage "wildlife" areas, even if the process of natural regeneration is too easily dominated by sycamore and buddleia. Squirrels may now be seen on Rush Common and even the occasional fox near Coldharbour Lane. Local birdlife now includes kestrels, blackbirds, robins, starlings, crows, magpies, wagtails and jays, and people are beginning to worry about the number of Canada geese in Brockwell Park!

The process of reclaiming Rush Common was begun back in the 1950s by the old Wandsworth Council, which laid out part as public open space in front of its Roupell Park Estate. After a period in which the LCC toyed with the idea of a massive road-widening of Brixton Hill, the work was eventually resumed by Lambeth using Urban Programme funds.

Not only were public sections opened up and enhanced, but communal garden areas like Josephine Avenue and Raleigh Gardens were also improved. The most recent addition is in front of 1-3 Effra Road, following the demolition of the old coach garage recently used as Brixton Fashion Centre.

7.4 Reviving the Centre

The riots of 1981 found Brixton probably at its lowest ebb, but despite the immediate damage, they generated a sense of urgency and some new thinking. Attempts were set in motion to brighten up the Town Centre, and to encourage new investment. By 1985, Lambeth Council's approach had shifted from painfully assembling large clearance areas to the marketing of individual sites. Nationally-known names began to return to the main shopping parades, and prominent sites like Bon Marche were brought back into full use. The street market is noticeably more active than 10 years ago.

Of course some of this is superficial, and mistakes have been made, but the regeneration has taken place despite the two severe recessions of 1981 and 1992, with very limited public resources.

Brixton cannot hope to regain its former status in terms of shopping volume, but its mass of small shops has great scope for speciality shopping. It still retains a distinctive Edwardian character which most other centres have lost in the course of rebuilding. Nowadays, all established high streets are under threat from the impact of drive-in supermarkets, out-of-centre warehouse stores and mail order shopping. Within London, there is the added problem of so many competing centres within the reach of a finite number of consumers.

Brixton's greatest potential seems to lie in its variety of venues for entertainment, leisure and the arts. During the 1970s many young people discovered Brixton as students or squatters, and those involved in arts, music and media are now strongly represented in the Brixton area. By the 1980s, some of them were showing interest in reviving several venues which survived from more prosperous times.

What had started in 1914 as the Palladium Cinema, next to the Town Hall, took on a new lease of life as The Fridge club and disco. The former Astoria cinema is now used for rock music concerts and rehearsals. However, a bid to re-open the defunct Empress Theatre for similar uses failed, and it was replaced by a block of flats.

The Ritzy Cinema was revived, initially as a modest art-house cinema, and more recently extended onto the former Brixton Theatre site to offer a choice of screens. Even St.Matthew's Church has been much altered internally to accommodate a wide range of uses, and now operates as The Brix, including a small theatre managed by the Shaw Theatre Company.

The old Ritzy Cinema restored as the centrepiece of a new development, 1995. After some 50 years of uncertainty, the old Brixton Theatre site was finally used for an extension to the Ritzy Cinema and some new flats. (Brixton Challenge)

APPENDIX -
REFERENCES AND FURTHER READING

1. RURAL BRIXTON:
Origins (and generally)
"Nature Conservation in Lambeth" ed. by Ian Yarham (Ecology Handbook 26, London Ecology Unit, 1994) includes a good general account of the development of Lambeth as a whole, with information on its topography and geology.

Saxon Hundred
The derivation of the place-name is discussed more fully in *"Brixton - the story of a name"* by Ken Dixon (Brixton Society, 1991).
See also *"The Place-names of Surrey"* (Oxford University Press, 1938).
Details of early Saxon settlements were kindly provided by Graham Gower, and since published in *"The Wandsworth Historian"* (Wandsworth Historical Society Journal, No.67, Spring 1995).

Manors & Estates
Domesday Book information is from the Surrey volume, translated by S.Wood and ed. by J.Morris (Phillimore, 1975).
The main source for early estates and residences is *"The Survey of London, Vol.26 - Lambeth (South)"* ed. by F.H.W.Sheppard (London County Council, 1956). This volume also details most of the families through whose hands the various estates passed.

The Rural Landscape
The River Effra is covered more fully in *"Effra - Lambeth's Underground River"* by Ken Dixon (Brixton Society, 1993).
The former use and management of South London's woodland is described in *"The Great North Wood"* by L.S.C.Neville (London Wildlife Trust: Southwark Group, 1987).
Some specimen lists of local taxpayers from ancient times were included in *"The History and Antiquities of Lambeth"* by John Tanswell (Frederick Picton, 1858).

Country Life on London's Fringe
Among the early maps held by Lambeth Archives Department, Milne's map of 1800 is notable for showing the boundaries and use of each field.
The two Brixton Windmills are described in detail in *"Windmills of Lambeth"* (Lambeth Council, c.1975).

Country Houses
The old Brockwell Hall and an Inquiry held there in 1563 are mentioned in *"Streatham Divided"* by Donald Imber (Streatham History Notes No.6, the Streatham Society, 1986). For obscure reasons, Lambeth Council sources refer to the present building as the *"Mansion House"*.

2. LEAFY SUBURB:
A Refuge from the City
As Clapham was already an established village with its own church, that side of Stockwell tended to develop first. Personalities associated with Clapham from the late 17th century onwards are featured in *"Clapham"* by Eric Smith (1976, reprinted by the Clapham Society).

The First Churches
Lambeth Archives has some early views of St.Andrew's as Stockwell Chapel including a couple of watercolours, c.1825.

Setting the Stage for Growth

Lambeth Archives hold a copy of the 1810 map of the Manor of Lambeth, recording the Inclosure Award. It also shows much detail of adjoining estates and their ownership.

Garden Suburbs

Much detail about the domestic arrangements of well-off families, or at least what they aspired to, can be found in early editions of *"Beeton's Book of Household Management"* by Isabella Beeton (1st edition 1861, facsimile reprint by Chancellor Press, 1984).

The Developers

"The Survey of London" Vol.26 (op.cit.) has been the main reference for ownership and development information in this chapter.

The story of William Roupell MP is set out more fully in *"The Roupells of Streatham Hill"* by Judy Harris (Streatham History Notes No.2, published by the Streatham Society, 1985).

Building a Community

Some local churches have published their own histories, notably *"A History of the Parish of St.Michael, Stockwell"* by Rev.Tony Lucas (St.Michael's Church, 1989) and at the opposite extremity of the district, *"Christ Church, Streatham - a History and Guide"* by Joan Payne (revised edition published by the Streatham Society, 1986). A number of shorter accounts, produced for church jubilees or centenaries, are held by Lambeth Archives.

The Brixton Lodge Academy opened on 15 January 1824 (advertisement in *"The Times"* of 19 January 1824, kindly supplied by Bill Linskey).

A fuller account of the Stockwell Educational Institute was compiled by Ken Dixon and published by the Brixton Society in 1993 as No.2 in the *"Brixton Abridged"* series.

An 1848 description of Brixton and its local institutions was also published in 1993, as No.3 in the *"Brixton Abridged"* series.

The House of Correction

Summarised from *"The Survey of London, Vol.26"* (op.cit.) with additional detail from *"The London Encyclopaedia"* ed. by Ben Weinreb and Christopher Hibbert (Macmillan, 1983).

Early Industry

Information on the water works kindly supplied by Geoffrey Saul of the Rickmansworth Historical Society.

3 . THE RAILWAY BOOM

The Railways Arrive

Additional information provided by Bill Marshall of the Peckham Society.

Terraces & Artisans' Dwellings

A good general study of Victorian terraced house designs is provided by *"The English Terraced House"* by Dr.Stefan Muthesius (c.1982).

The origin of the *"Poets"* roads is recorded in *"The Survey of London"* Vol.26 (op cit.). The dates of other houses around Railton Road were researched in 1974, mainly using old drainage records held by Lambeth Council's then Borough Engineer. Several leases recently deposited in Lambeth Archives appear to confirm the dates for development of the Effra Hall Estate.

Specimen Census entry obtained by Mark Frankel and first published in the Brixton Society Newsletter (No.55, January 1982).

Victorian Street Names

Reprints of the early large-scale Ordnance Survey maps, from 1870 onwards, identifying not only street names but some individual house names, are published by Alan Godfrey of Gateshead, and available through the Brixton Society. Lambeth Archives holds an extensive collection of old street maps and directories.

Omnibus & Tram

For fuller details of services see *"Trams in Brixton 1870-1951"* by Ken Dixon (Brixton Abridged series No.1, Brixton Society, 1993).
Information on early bus services was also provided by Ken Dixon.

Church & Chapel

The Torrey & Alexander Mission was erected for an evangelical campaign c. 1905. See contemporary reports in the *"South London Press"* and *"Brixton Memories"*, p12. For a thorough study of the social work of local churches, see *"The English Churches in a Secular Society - Lambeth 1870-1930"* by Jeffrey Cox (Oxford University Press, 1982).

The Victorians at Leisure

A new complication in research is the recent vogue for revamping old-established public houses under new names. Additional material on music hall artistes may be found in Lambeth Archives.

Public Parks & Gardens

The origin of each public open space in Lambeth is recounted in *"Lambeth's Open Spaces - An Historical Account"* by Marie Draper (Lambeth Council, 1979).

4 . RISE OF THE SHOPPING CENTRE

Population Pressures & Market Forces

This chapter (particularly this section) is based on a talk by Alan Piper at the Lambeth Archives Open Day, September 1992.

The Victorian Shopkeeper

The Ordnance Survey map reprints from Alan Godfrey (op.cit.) include on the back, extracts from local directories, giving some idea of the number and mix of shops and tradesmen.
Brian Bloice, of Southwark and Lambeth Archaeological Society, has researched the Axtens family and other early residents of Leigham Court Road, Streatham.

The Big Stores Arrive

The development of David Greig's chain of provision shops is summarised in *"David Greig - the Story of a Family Firm"* published by the company in 1970. For more detail, see a volume of memoirs by David Greig's wife, privately printed in the 1930s, and held by Lambeth Archives.

More than just Shopping

Many postcard views of Central Brixton around this time are included in *"Brixton and Norwood in Old Photographs"* by Jill Dudman (Alan Sutton Publishing, 1995). Some of the more prominent entertainment buildings are the subject of postcard reprints published by the Brixton Society.
Profiles of the two theatres are included in *"Lambeth's Theatrical Heritage"* by John Cresswell (Streatham Society, 1991). Information on early cinemas was also provided by John Cresswell as part of a talk to the Brixton Society, 24 September 1990. Several reminiscences of Brixton cinemas are included in *"Enter the Dream House"* ed. by M.O'Brien & A.Eyles (Museum of the Moving Image 1991).

Interwar Investment
Dates of individual stores have been collected from a variety of sources, including *"The Gazette of the John Lewis Partnership"* Vol.57 No.19, 7 June 1975.
Street Market & Arcades
The quotation is from *"The Brixton Free Press Almanac for 1889"*, with further detail from notes compiled by a Mr Peter Moore in 1964 and lodged in the Tate Reference Library, Brixton.

5. SOCIAL CHANGE
A Metropolitan Role
Parish Vestry information is from the *"Lambeth Official Guide"* p.27-8 (Pyramid Press, 1953/54). For London-wide services, see *"Achievement - a short history of the LCC"* by W.Eric Jackson (Longmans, 1965).

Promoting Local Health
A fuller account of the Brixton Dispensary, by Mary Lightfoot, was given in Brixton Society Newsletter No.98, September 1988. *"The Brixton Free Press Almanac 1889"* describes its mode of operation at that time.

Extending Education
A brief account of the "Stockwell Murder" of 1871 was compiled by Mark Frankel and appeared in Brixton Society Newsletter No.53, October 1981. The case is explored at length in *"Watson's Apology"* by Beryl Bainbridge (Duckworth, 1984).

The School of Building
"The First Fifty Years" outlines the early days of the Brixton School of Building (London County Council, 1954).

Electrifying Transport
Underground railway information mainly from *"The London Encyclopaedia"* (op.cit.). *"The South London Line"* (Middleton Press, 1995) depicts rail stations and services early in the century. Information on Tram services from *"Trams in Brixton 1870-1951"* (op.cit.)

Eminent Edwardians
Information chiefly from *"The Dictionary of National Biography"* (in Brixton Reference Library). Van Gogh's early years in England are covered in *"Young Vincent"* by Martin Bailey (W.H.Allen, 1990).

The First World War
Information on war damage from Lambeth Archives, kindly researched by Doreen Heath of the Lambethans Society. Details of public transport changes provided by Bill Marshall of the Peckham Society.

Housing Changes
Several reminiscences of Brixton life, particularly in the 1930s, have been published in *"Brixton Memories"* compiled by Ken Dixon (Brixton Society, 1994).

Commerce & Industry
Information on the Sunlight Laundry from Nicholas Long of the 20th Century Society.

War Damage
Figures for air raid damage are from the Lambeth Official Guide, 1953/54 (op.cit.). There are extensive Civil Defence records in Lambeth Archives, yet to be fully explored.
A typical design of a deep shelter on the Northern Line was illustrated in *"Building Design"* magazine, 20 September 1985, p.60 and reprinted in Brixton Society Newsletter No.121, July 1992.

6 . INTO DECLINE

The Housing Crisis

Memories of post-war immigrants from the Caribbean were published as *"Forty Winters On"* by the South London Press and The Voice, 1988.

"Lambeth Interface" by Cedric Jackson (privately published, 1975) provides a personal but nevertheless thorough insight into Housing, Planning and Community issues around Brixton in the early 1970s.

Local concerns are also evident in the newsletters of several neighbourhood councils and other community groups (Lambeth Archives, ephemera collection, file 555).

Decline of the Shopping Centre

Successive proposals for the Town Centre are described in a long series of Lambeth Council committee reports, c.1963-1987, which should all be accessible in Lambeth Archives.

Political Life

Details of Brixton's MPs were researched by Hugh Barclay and first published in Brixton Society Newsletter No.119, March 1992.

Potted biographies of John Major appeared in several newspapers following his appointment as Prime Minister in November 1990, with the fullest account of his local connections in the South London Press, 30 November 1990, p.8-9. See also *"The Major Enigma"* by Penny Junor (Michael Joseph, 1993).

Information on Ken Livingstone from press cuttings in Lambeth Archives, notably The Times (14.2.83, p.8) and South London Press (4.5.84, p.5).

Troubled Times

The Report of Lord Scarman's Inquiry *"The Brixton Disorders, 10-12 April 1981"* (HMSO, Cmnd.8427, November 1981) includes a detailed account of the riots over that weekend.

7 . NEW DIRECTIONS

Finding a Way Forward

This chapter draws on various papers in my possession, from Lambeth Council, Brixton Challenge and other bodies, which may not all be available in Lambeth Archives yet.

The original series of Inner Area Studies was published by HMSO in 1977. Voluntary Sector participation in Lambeth's *"Inner City Partnership"* was co-ordinated by the Lambeth Inner City Consultative Group. Brixton Challenge has published an updated Action Programme each year, including objectives, organisation, and key statistical and financial information.

The Scarman Report & After

A more extended summary of policing developments since 1981 was included in *"The Vauxhall View"*, No.29, pages 1-10 (Steve Morse. February 1996).

Life Returns

See also *"Nature Conservation in Lambeth"* (op.cit.).

Reviving the Centre

The launch or re-opening of each venue has received good coverage in the local press. *"Brixton Village"* Magazine No.2, February 1993, included a feature on the Brixton Academy (p.10-11) and a report on completion of the new flats on the Empress site (p.5).

A BRIEF INDEX

Rear cover photos (Richard Barnatt, Brixton Challenge):

Left: A recent view of the street market in Electric Avenue, without the original cast iron canopy over the shopfronts.
Centre: St. Matthew's Church, now The Brix, as seen from Effra Road.
Right: The Atlantic public house, now the Dogstar, on the corner of Atlantic Road and Coldharbour Lane.